CHRISTIAN ENCOUNTERS

GALILEO

CHRISTIAN ENCOUNTERS

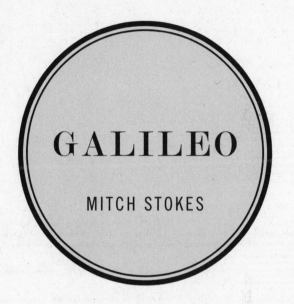

GALILEO

MITCH STOKES

THOMAS NELSON

Since 1798

NASHVILLE DALLAS MEXICO CITY RIO DE JANEIRO

Published in Nashville, Tennessee, by Thomas Nelson. Thomas Nelson is a registered trademark of Thomas Nelson, Inc.

Thomas Nelson, Inc., titles may be purchased in bulk for educational, business, fund-raising, or sales promotional use. For information, please e-mail SpecialMarkets@ThomasNelson.com.

Library of Congress Cataloging-in-Publication Data

Stokes, Mitch.
  Galileo / by Mitch Stokes.
    p. cm. — (Christian encounters)
  Includes bibliographical references.
  ISBN 978-1-59555-031-6
  1. Galilei, Galileo, 1564–1642 2. Astronomers—Italy—Biography. 3. Physicists—Italy—Biography. I. Title.
  QB36.G2S87 2011
  520.92—dc22
  [B]

                              2010036604

                    Printed in the United States of America
                    11 12 13 14 15 HCI 6 5 4 3 2 1

FOR CHRISTINE,
AN ASTOUNDING WOMAN

CONTENTS

PREFACE

It appears to me, that they who rely simply on the weight of authority to prove any assertion, without searching out the arguments to support it, act absurdly. I wish to question freely and to answer freely without any sort of adulation. That well becomes any who are sincere in the search for truth.[1]

This heroic passage—written by Galileo's father, Vincenzio—appears in many biographies of Galileo.[2] Its sentiment, we are frequently told, was Galileo's inheritance. As one biographer eloquently put it, "His father's revolt against authority was not lost on young Galileo. Skepticism permeated the Galilei household . . . To be liberated from authority became the longing of the son as well."[3]

This is the Galileo we know, an individualistic man of science, daringly opposed to all authority but his own. And tragically, martyrdom was his hero's reward. But like those of many martyrs, Galileo's sufferings have given those who have taken up his cause the courage to stand firm in a storm of benighted oppression. Especially benighted religious oppression.

This is indeed a stirring image of Galileo, one that has inspired plays, television specials, and even an opera. But, just

1

like Vincenzio's passage above, this portrait of Galileo is histori-
cally inaccurate. Facts have an annoying way of disappointing.

In the case of Vincenzio's quotation, we now know that it
was altered from the original, perhaps unintentionally, but just
enough to make it entirely misleading.[4] The corrected passage
shows that Vincenzio was merely arguing that when we have a
dispute about a matter of ordinary sense experience, we should
consult our own experience whenever we can.[5] What's more,
Vincenzio the antiauthoritarian supported his view with a frank
appeal to authority, namely, Aristotle's.[6] He went on to say, "I
speak of natural and ordinary things humanly and not of super-
natural and divine things."[7] When it came to topics like religion
and history, he believed, we *should* appeal to authority.[8]

Galileo's biographers are therefore quite right: Vincenzio
did bequeath his view of authority to his Galileo. But because
of his heritage, Galileo never once balked at the authority of
the Church, even when he could safely do so.

In fact, near the end of his life, Galileo counted his own zeal
for the Church as one of his greatest consolations. Regarding his
condemnation by the Catholic Church, Galileo wrote privately
to a friend:

> This afflicts me less than people may think possible, for I have
> two sources of perpetual comfort—first, that in my writ-
> ings there cannot be found the faintest shadow of irreverence
> towards the Holy Church; and second, the testimony of my
> own conscience, which only I and God in Heaven thoroughly
> know. And He knows that in this cause for which I suffer,

though many might have spoken with more learning, none,
not even the ancient Fathers, have spoken with more piety or
with greater zeal for the Church than I.[9]

Notice that Galileo said that his suffering was for the sake of a
"cause." This cause was not that of Copernicanism or even of
science in general. Rather, says the Galilean historian Stillman
Drake, "The cause for which Galileo suffered, in his own view,
was clearly not Copernicanism but sound theology and Christian
zeal."[10] Drake goes on to say:

> Galileo's own conscience was clear both as Catholic and as
> scientist. On one occasion he wrote, almost in despair, that
> at times he felt like burning all his work in science but he
> never so much as thought of turning his back on his faith.[11]

Galileo, we are surprised to hear, was a devout Christian, and
his debate with theologians was an internal Catholic debate
over the interpretation of Scripture. It was never—again we
are shocked—a debate between a proponent of secular science
on the one hand and the adherents of religious faith on the
other.

But to see this, we can't ignore the details of Galileo's life
and scientific work. For one thing, "the Galileo affair," as it is
now called, resulted largely from an ignorance of mathematics
and science. This fact should give us considerable pause—
today, widespread avoidance of math and science is cliché. For
another thing, the myths that have grown around the Galileo

affair—especially the myth that science and religion are natural enemies—have been the result of a convenient neglect of facts.

The paradox is this: Galileo's story, as it has come to us, is at once clouded and stripped bare. And to get an accurate picture of the Galileo affair, we must study more than isolated and impersonal facts; we must study a life.

FROM MONKS
TO MEDICINE

According to Italian custom, we know Galileo by his first name. This was an honor conferred upon him even in his own lifetime; he was one of a kind, requiring only his first name to single him out. He belongs to that special group of Italians who have contributed not only to Italy's splendor, but to our race's: Dante, Michelangelo, Raphael, and, nearer our own time, Madonna. But Galileo's first name is also his last. Galileo Galilei. And perhaps a man with two first names need only go by one of them.

Galileo could trace his ancestry back to the 1200s, to a Florentine who had not a single "Galileo" to his name: Giovanni Bonaiuti.[1] But Giovanni's great-grandson, *Galileo* Bonaiuti was a man of distinction, an official at the University of Florence and a professor of medicine. And he wasn't a mere academic. He had a successful medical practice, though given the state of health care in that time, success was measured on a curve.

Bonaiuti also had a distinguished political career as a member of Florence's governing council. Being involved in city government was substantially more impressive in Renaissance Italy than being, say, a mayor or city counselor today. Cities were the most powerful political entities in Italy: Venice, Florence, and, of course, Rome. Italy, in truth, didn't even exist during this time. The Italian state wouldn't be created until 1861. Italy was simply the boot-shaped landmass jutting into the Mediterranean, controlled by a number of duchies and republics, each looking out for itself.

Galileo Bonaiuti's achievements were considerable; therefore, when he died around 1450, a proud relative considered Galileo worthy enough to be the founder of a new and eminent Florentine family.[2] On Bonaiuti's tombstone, this relative inscribed *Galileis de Galilei, at one time Bonaiutis*. The name stuck. Both of them.

Eighty years later, in 1520, the Galilei family was still distinguished, although its financial station, if not its pedigree, had declined significantly. In this year, Vincenzio Galilei was born in Florence. Vincenzio, and his son Galileo—*our* Galileo— would always be proud of their citizenry, and Galileo would refer to himself as "a noble Florentine" on his books' title pages.

The Galileis were justifiably pleased with their Florentine background. Florence, the "Flourishing Town," was the seat of the Renaissance in northern Italy, particularly during the 1400s, the *Quattrocento*. It was the home of Dante, Leonardo da Vinci, Machiavelli, and Michelangelo. In recent years, it had been one of the most powerful cities in Europe, the home of rich and influential cloth makers and bankers. Its currency, the florin, was a world monetary standard. Even America is something of a Florentine product, named after Florence's own Amerigo Vespucci.

Vincenzio Galilei was a talented musician, so talented, in fact, that he attracted the attention of the famed Giovanni Bardi.[3] Bardi was the patron of the Florentine *Camerata*, a group of prominent musical and literary intelligentsia whose efforts eventually (and unfortunately) produced opera.[4] Bardi funded Vincenzio's study of music theory under the Venetian master Gioseffo Zarlino. Vincenzio's time with Zarlino would be important for the history of music; it was Vincenzio's disagreement with his teacher over music theory that would prompt him to write his *Dialogue on Ancient and Modern Music*, a work known throughout Europe, and one that even the astronomer Johannes Kepler quoted with approval.[5]

In addition to music, Vincenzio was a decent mathematician and used this ability in the service of music theory. This might surprise us, but music was one of the ancient Pythagorean divisions of mathematics (along with arithmetic, geometry, and astronomy). Pythagoras, a Greek mathematician and mystic, formed a religious brotherhood revolving around the belief that the world is fundamentally mathematical. And for reasons unknown, he prohibited the brothers from eating beans. The close association between mathematics and music (but not beans) is probably why Kepler was familiar with Vincenzio's work. Kepler was a zealous Pythagorean and believed at one time that the planets' mathematically governed movements actually produced music—the harmony of the spheres.

Vincenzio, however, was unable to support himself solely

by teaching and performing. He therefore took up another respectable Florentine tradition—he became a cloth merchant, specializing in wool. The lute would have to take second place to wool, in practice, if not in Vincenzio's heart.

After Vincenzio finished his music studies in Venice in 1561 or 1562, he traveled to Pisa to trade wool.[6] One of his friends and business contacts—Muzio Tedaldi—probably introduced Vincenzio to his cousin, Giulia Ammannati. We know very little about Giulia, and what we do know isn't flattering; she has been described as prickly, quarrelsome, willful, and difficult.[7] But there is, no doubt, more to the story, and Vincenzio and Giulia were married in July 1562 in Pisa. Part of Giulia's dowry was linen and wool cloth.

The couple settled in the countryside near Pisa, where Vincenzio established a small music school in the house of a noble family.[8] But he still depended on cloth trading, although neither trading nor teaching provided much income, even when combined. But at least the ends met.

~

Pisa, like the city of Florence, lies along the Arno River in the region of Tuscany. Since 1406, Pisa had belonged to Florence, and the powerful Medici family now controlled both. Unlike Florence, however, Pisa is on the low-lying western coast rather than in the foothills of Italy's spinelike Apennines. At one time, Pisa had been a coastal town, but deposits from the Arno moved the coast a few miles to the west. Pisa's soil was still soft and marshy, requiring builders to take care. Not all of them did.

The Leaning Tower of Pisa is the campanile—the freestanding bell tower—of Pisa's cathedral. In the cathedral's baptistry, on February 19, 1564, Vincenzio and Giulia baptized their first child, four days after he was born. Vincenzio had named the child after the founder of the Galilean line, hoping little Galileo's story would restore the family's splendor. And indeed, the boy's story would become legendary, even the precarious bell tower part of that legend. But in 1564, Galileo's story was just beginning. That same year saw the birth of Shakespeare and the deaths of Michelangelo and John Calvin.

We know very little about Galileo's childhood, but some things are clear. In 1572, when he was eight, his father moved back to Florence—now the seat of the Duchy of Tuscany—leaving the boy and his mother in Pisa to live with Tedaldi. Financially strapped people commonly asked relatives to temporarily care for wives and children while they ordered their finances. Two years later, in 1574, Galileo and his mother were reunited with Vincenzio in the Tuscan capital.

In Florence, Galileo learned Latin and Greek from his father and a few tutors. His curriculum also included the fine arts, and he became an excellent lute player, organist, and singer. Painting, too, was included. Later in life, Galileo told friends that if he could choose his career over again, he would become a painter.[9] Cigoli, a well-known artist, said that Galileo had trained him on visual perspective and that this training was responsible for his own fame.[10]

Literature, especially poetry, enamored Galileo. And although he would become famous primarily for mathematics and science,

Galileo's love of words would change the style of Italian literature. Leonardo Oskchki says, "In the period between Machiavelli and Manzoni, Galileo is the master of Italian prose as well as the creator of its classical style; to discover the roots of subsequent Italian prose one must seek them in Galileo's writings."[11] Galileo's scientific writings were works of art.

The boy was gifted, and soon Vincenzio had taught Galileo all he could. Sometime after 1574—we don't know exactly when—Vincenzio sent Galileo to be educated at the mysterious monastery in Vallombrosa, the "Valley of Shadows." The monastery—a congregation of Benedictine monks located in the Apennine mountains—was later made famous by John Milton's reference to it in *Paradise Lost*.

Depending on when Galileo arrived at Vallombrosa, he stayed there as long as four years. The monks gave him an exceptional education, based on the medieval curriculum of the trivium: grammar, logic, and rhetoric. Galileo apparently loved it. In 1579, when he was fifteen, he joined the order as a novice, an official prospect. He immediately began his novitiate—his probationary period, which would last a year or two—receiving his novice's habit, the telltale hooded robe. Once he successfully completed his probation, he would take his vows and receive a brother's habit. Galileo had chosen his path.

He apparently had not cleared the choice with his father. On Vincenzio's next visit to Vallombrosa, he immediately brought Galileo back to Florence. The reason, Vincenzio said, was that Galileo's eyes needed attention that the monks could not provide. And it was true: Galileo suffered from opthamalia. Whether this was Vincenzio's actual reason, we don't know. The decision could have been financial. Vincenzio was in no position to afford the down payment and upkeep for a religious vocation that earned no income.[12] In any case, Galileo never returned.

He continued, however, to study with Vallombrosian monks, only now in Florence and not as a prospective member of the order.[13] Vincenzio's career plans for Galileo were becoming plain, at least to Vincenzio. Galileo was extraordinarily intelligent. He was also good with his hands; besides painting and music, Galileo busied himself with woodworking. Generations earlier, the family had become great, in part, because of the first Galileo's celebrated medical career. This seemed the perfect profession for his namesake. Galileo, his father determined, would become a doctor. It was not the last time a father would be disappointed.

2

AN ADVANCED
CIVILIZATION

Unfortunately, very few parents could afford a university education for their young men. And although Vincenzio was not as poor as many Italians, he was not in any position to pay for Galileo's tuition, room, and board. The Galilei family had grown in the seventeen years since Galileo was born; Galileo was only one of seven children.

But there was hope. The University of Pisa had a government-supported residential college—the *Collegio della Sapienza*—dedicated to needy but promising Tuscans. If a Tuscan resident could show that he was in need and could pass a Latin exam, he could apply for one of forty prestigious spots in the college.[1] If he was awarded one of the scholarships, he would receive tuition and board for up to six years. In return, the student swore an oath of fealty to the Tuscan grand duke (who at this time was Francesco de' Medici). It was a fabulous arrangement but highly competitive. Students would apply year after year, most of them entirely unsuccessful—like Galileo.

There was, however, one last ray of hope. The Galileis' relative Muzio Tedaldi still lived in Pisa, and he had offered to have Galileo live with his family if the scholarship fell through. This was a generous offer, especially in those times, and it would relieve Vincenzio just enough to pay for tuition. So in the fall of 1581, Galileo moved from Florence to Pisa and enrolled in the University as an *artista*, a student of medicine and philosophy.[2] Tedaldi had helped the Galileis before, and their debt to him was sizable. But what was family for, after all?

~

The University of Pisa's medical faculty was part of the faculty of arts, which also included philosophy and mathematics.[3] But medicine still held pride of place. Philosophy was seen merely as preparation for medical training. And mathematics was all but neglected. There was only one lonely mathematics professor in the entire university (Filippo Fantoni, a Camaldolese monk), and he was paid in proportion to his subject's esteem, which was very little indeed.[4] Medical students avoided mathematics like the plague they would unsuccessfully treat.

The medical curriculum itself consisted primarily of the ancient physicians Hippocrates and Galen. The preparatory philosophical training, however, was an overview of European science, which meant Aristotelian physics and cosmology. This part of philosophy—what we call *science*—was called *natural philosophy*, not to contrast it with the unnatural kind, but to indicate that it was the study of nature.

It may be surprising that the science of the medieval and Renaissance universities was largely Aristotelian, given the centrality of Christianity in Europe. Aristotle was a pagan, after all. But this, the scholars of the time would say, is to assume a false dichotomy. Aristotle and Christianity, they believed, accorded quite well on many important issues. This alleged accord is particularly important for understanding the great controversies in Galileo's life. Aristotelianism had become so entwined with Christian doctrine that it was difficult to tell where Christianity ended and Aristotelianism began. Furthermore, this system of Aristotle-plus-Christianity—called *Scholasticism* because it originated in the medieval universities or "schools" (*scholae*)—was a powerfully coherent picture of the world. Pull one thread and watch the entire thing unravel.

So then, as part of the university's medical curriculum, Galileo immediately and dutifully began to study philosophy. And he enjoyed it immensely. Little did he know, however, that it would eventually involve him in a revolution in natural philosophy, a scientific revolution—*the* scientific revolution. Over the course of the next century or so, Aristotle's rule would crumble, the coup culminating in the mathematical physics of Isaac Newton. But at this time, there was no indication that there was even going to *be* a revolution. Although nearly forty years earlier, in 1543, Nicolaus Copernicus had planted the seeds of one, it remained dormant, waiting to be awakened by Galileo.

But for now, it was time for Galileo to learn from Aristotle, not to overthrow him.

~

Centuries earlier, as the glory of Rome faded, so did the quality and quantity of learning, especially scientific learning. By the time of the Muslim invasions during the seventh century AD, European scientific activity had nearly ceased. Europeans, in their struggle simply to survive, had lost their leisure, and so the luxury of learning. They had also lost most of the documents and traditions of ancient Greece. Although these centuries weren't entirely dark, there was very little light from classical and Hellenistic antiquity. Christianity alone sustained Europe's smoldering intellectual fire.

But by the 900s, Europe was slowly gathering its economic and political strength. As trading grew, so did contact with Muslim learning, which consisted mostly of ancient Greek texts and their various commentaries. These were eventually translated from Arabic into Latin, culminating in what is sometimes called Europe's Twelfth Century Renaissance.[5] The communities that gathered to study these texts became the world's first universities.

Because the men of Europe had remained for so long in the dark, the light from the ancient texts nearly blinded them. We tend to scoff at the knowledge of the ancients. But it would be difficult to overstate the genius, creativity, subtlety, and coherence of ancient knowledge, particularly knowledge of the natural world. And medieval Europe had unexpectedly discovered an advanced civilization.

This awe lasted for centuries, continuing as the myth of "ancient wisdom." In addition to the great things that Europe had actually found, there was speculation of much more— a vast store of learning, hardly to be imagined. Even Newton believed in such a storehouse of knowledge; part of the motivation behind his incomparable discoveries was his belief that he was rediscovering knowledge that mankind had lost. He even believed that the ancient Greeks had known about calculus.

Europe's astonishment on encountering the ancient texts created a unique intellectual culture, one highly respectful of ancient Greek authority. This was only reasonable. If today we unearthed documents from an extremely advanced culture, we would take them very seriously. And so Europe did. In fact, they expended most of their intellectual effort on simply recovering and consolidating the ancient wisdom.

Aristotle's work was particularly prized. No other ancient thinker had constructed such an expansive, coherent, and impressive system of thought. Aristotle's comprehensive system included such apparently disparate disciplines as logic, rhetoric, poetry, ethics, physics, zoology, cosmology, and metaphysics. Throughout the Middle Ages, Aristotle was often simply called "the Philosopher"; there were no competitors. The twentieth century's most eminent Galileo scholar, Stillman Drake, distills the European mind-set this way:

> If one wished to *know*, the way to go about it was to read the texts of Aristotle with care, to study commentaries on Aristotle in order to grasp his meaning in difficult passages,

and to explore questions that had been raised and debated arising from Aristotle's books . . . [All] matters of knowledge belonged to Philosophy just as all matters of faith belonged to Sacred Theology.[6]

A corollary of this mind-set—or perhaps an assumption supporting it—was that there are two separate domains of study: knowledge and faith. The source of the first is reason and sense perception. The second comes from God himself, in the form of Scripture and the teachings of his church. The two domains are entirely compatible, the scholastics acknowledged. But heaven help those who inadvertently mixed them.

EVERYTHING IN ITS
RIGHT PLACE

K nowledge of the physical universe—knowledge of the cosmos—was considered philosophical knowledge and therefore knowledge of Aristotle's universe. He was *the* Philosopher, after all. And without at least a sketchy understanding of Aristotelian science, any recounting of Galileo's saga will be a caricature. For most of Galileo's life, his difficulties would come from the academic philosophers—the scientists—not from the Catholic Church. In fact, the scientists themselves were largely responsible for the Church's involvement. Moreover, Galileo's discoveries—and the resistance they incited—make no sense whatsoever without knowing *how* they were new.

At its most basic, Aristotle's universe is spherical, the earth resting comfortably at its center. The universe's outer boundary is an enormous crystalline sphere in which the stars are embedded. This outer sphere—this bejeweled hamster ball—is emphatically *not* at rest; it rotates at a dizzying speed, completing its journey once every day.

To picture the universe this way demands little imagination. In fact, to think of it any other way requires us to suppress the most evident interpretation of our senses. There are very few things more obvious than a stationary earth. And it is only slightly less obvious that the stars are part of a transparent sphere that rotates around us. For most of human history, it would have been unreasonable to believe otherwise, requiring a certain touch of madness. Or genius.

In addition to the fixed stars, there are other celestial bodies, the most obvious being the sun and moon. According to Aristotle, both of these are fixed in their own thick, crystalline shells. These shells also rotated around the earth—the sun's once a day, the moon's taking an hour longer. In addition, there are five "wandering stars" apparently detached from the outer sphere, all set in their own shells. The Greeks called these *planets*, their word for "wanderer." The earth, in Aristotle's view, is not a planet, but like you, an object entirely unique.

The universe, then, is a series of concentric or nested shells, not unlike a set of spherical Russian nesting dolls with an earthy core. God, or the "prime mover," moves the outermost sphere, and because all the spheres are in contact with their neighbors, the movement of the outermost sphere of fixed stars is transferred to each subsequent sphere.

The moon is closest to the earth, and so its shell is the smallest, the first sphere we encounter as we travel outward toward the stars. The moon's shell is special because it divides the universe into two very different realms. Below the moon's sphere is the sublunary or *terrestrial* realm. Beyond the lunar sphere is the heavenly or *celestial* realm. These two realms are composed of different material and subject to very different laws. The universe, according to Aristotle, is segregated. Everything is in its right place.

~

The terrestrial realm is where change and corruption occur, where mankind—the epitome of change and corruption—resides. Everything in the sublunary realm, including humans, is made of some combination of the four elements: earth, air, fire, and water (these were first proposed by Empedocles a century before Aristotle).[1]

Each element has its own essential characteristics, its own fundamental *essence* or *nature*. Natures, according to Aristotle, are strange, mysterious things that make each object just what it is. More than that, it's difficult to say. Natures are perhaps a sort of physical blueprint or programming. Or maybe they're something like a definition, materially manifested. None of these metaphors is quite right. But regardless of their spookiness, regardless of what natures *are*, what they *do* is more important. Each object's nature dictates how it behaves.

In the case of the four elements, each—*by nature*—has a place of rest that it "desires" to reach. What makes earth the heaviest element is that its natural place is the very center of the universe. When it is unrestricted, earth will move toward its ideal central location; it will "fall." Fire, on the other hand, is the lightest element; its natural place of rest is just under the moon's celestial sphere. This is why fire rises. Air is the next lightest element and will always try to reach its natural place just inside that of fire's sphere. Water's natural place lies between air and earth.

But the constant rotational motion of the moon's shell stirs up the terrestrial realm, mixing the four elements, which is why the terrestrial world isn't structured as four nested shells of earth, water, air, and fire. A rock, for example, is made mostly of earth, but also contains a tiny bit of other elements. But because of the rock's vast proportion of earth, it will travel toward its natural destination if unhindered (if dropped, say). The earth (our home) is located at the center of the cosmos for this very reason—it is composed mostly of earth (the element), which has congregated around its natural place. This is where it is supposed to be.

Each object's nature determines not only *where* it wants to naturally go, but also *how* it will get there. In other words, all terrestrial objects have a *natural* motion, a motion dictated by their nature. This natural motion is simple: every sublunary object naturally moves in a straight line, either directly toward or directly away from the center of the universe. A dropped rock moves *straight* toward the center of the earth because it is mostly earth.

In Aristotle's terrestrial physics, a rock's downward motion—its falling—is not caused by an *external force* like gravity. Nothing is pulling on the rock. Rather, the cause of the rock's motion is *in* the rock; its motion is caused by its nature or essence. An analogy from the animate world is particularly useful here, for Aristotle's physics takes cues from organisms.

Imagine your cat chasing a bird. The cat moves entirely on its own; there is no external force being physically applied to it. The cat moves in the direction(s) it does—and at the speed it does—because it wants to. The cause of the cat's motion is *inside* it, beneath its skin.

Aristotle didn't believe that rocks were literally alive; rather, animate objects provided a helpful metaphor or model for inanimate objects. We now apply the metaphor of a machine—especially a clock—to the universe. But for Aristotle, the world was akin to a living thing.

≈

Not all motion in the terrestrial realm, however, is natural or unhindered. Sometimes terrestrial objects *don't* move toward their natural resting place. When you *pick up* a rock, it moves away from the earth's center, and so its motion is *un*natural. Therefore, its motion isn't caused by its nature. Rather, it is caused by *you*. Instead of being moved by an internal force, the rock is moved by the *external* force that your hand applies through physical contact. Unnatural motion was called "violent" motion, a description deriving from the Latin word for "force." It is also called, less interestingly, "forced" motion.

For Aristotle, all motion—natural or violent—requires an explanation. In other words, something must *cause* an object to move. This seems obvious enough. If you stop pulling a wagon, it stops moving. And according to Aristotle, as we have seen, motion has two kinds of causes. In the case of natural motion, the explanation is always the object's internal nature; violent motion is always caused by an external force. Rest, on the other hand, requires no cause at all; there's nothing to explain.

But it was quickly realized—even in Aristotle's day—that *thrown* rocks, for example, provided a stiff challenge for Aristotelian physics. Notice that if you throw a rock horizontally, the rock's motion is not (at first) toward the center of the earth and therefore can't be explained by its internal nature. The only other possible cause of its horizontal motion is an external force. But it was believed that an external force could only be applied by physical contact (science is no longer so sure about this). The question then becomes, what causes the rock's motion *after* it leaves your hand and *before* it naturally falls to the ground? Our own answer to this simple question—which Galileo bequeathed to us—is the cornerstone of modern physics. And it is absolutely mystifying, as we will see.

But Aristotle's answer is somewhat disappointing. This isn't surprising. In his physics, Aristotle was interested in *nature*, which is just what the word *physics* means. Violent or forced motion is *un*natural, and so not part of nature, strictly speaking.

Nevertheless, Aristotle halfheartedly attempted an explanation. And despite its troubles, it is, oddly, more believable than the truth. Aristotle said that once the rock leaves your hand, the air behind it pushes it forward. That is, during the rock's travel through the air, some of the air rushes in behind the rock to fill the empty space left in the rock's wake. The air moves to fill that space because nature, according to Aristotle, will do whatever it can to avoid a vacuum. This principle is called *horror vacuii*— "nature abhors a vacuum."[2]

By the Middle Ages, philosophers had replaced Aristotle's dubious explanation of violent motion. When we throw a rock, the medievals said, a driving force—an *impetus*—is transferred from our hand to the rock. In other words, the external force that we initially provide becomes an internal force in the rock, a force that gradually dies out as the rock travels through the air. As the impetus decays, the rock's nature takes over, moving it to the ground.

The impetus theory, then, was a halfway house between Aristotle's view and our own theory of *inertia*. The proponents of the impetus theory agreed with Aristotle that all motion requires a cause. Today we do not believe this because we believe in inertia. According to our own contemporary physics—what we consider to be the truth of the matter—there *is* no force causing a thrown rock to move horizontally through the air after it leaves your hand. Once a rock is moving forward, it will continue moving forward because of its inertia, which is its *tendency to continue doing what it's doing*. In modern physics, neither rest nor motion requires a cause; causes are only needed for a *change* in motion (i.e., speeding up, slowing down, changing direction, starting, and stopping). To put it somewhat differently, an object will keep doing what it's doing unless an external force causes it to do something else.

The famous historian of science Herbert Butterfield once said that the concept of inertia is the most important intellectual hurdle of the last fifteen hundred years.[3] It is also the cornerstone of modern physics and will make its appearance later in Galileo's story. Despite inertia's importance, it is no less mysterious than

Aristotelian natures. Calling inertia a "tendency" doesn't tell us what it is; it only provides comfort, like attaching a name to a mysterious disease. Other than its name, we have no idea what inertia *is*.

~

Whereas Aristotle's terrestrial realm is complicated and corruptible, his celestial realm is simple and immutable. It is composed of a single element. This fifth element or essence—this quintessence—is called "aether." In contrast to the straight-line natural motion of the four terrestrial elements, aether naturally moves in circles. This is why the celestial orbs or shells rotate—it is simply in their nature, and so we can't really blame them. And because nothing stops them, they rotate eternally.

It is natural, at this point, to ask what is outside the universe, what is beyond the ethereal sphere of the fixed stars? Aristotle's answer is as astonishing as it is unimaginable: there is nothing at all, not even space. There isn't even a "beyond": beyondness is a spatial concept.

Despite its strangeness to modern minds, Aristotle's natural philosophy is far more intuitive than our own. It is also remarkably coherent. Even with the Aristotelian universe's uncompromising segregation, it is difficult to modify any single feature of Aristotle's philosophy without affecting the entire system. A change in the cosmic structure would do irreparable damage to terrestrial physics. Displace the earth from its central position, for example, and the explanation for why heavy objects fall vanishes. And that, Galileo would discover, would be only the beginning of the trouble.

4

THE SEDUCTION

During Galileo's time at Pisa, Aristotelian philosophy absorbed him as much as he absorbed it. But Galileo wasn't entirely passive, uncritically accepting everything his professors taught. In fact, Galileo earned a reputation for being obstinate. Perhaps he questioned his teachers on points they thought unreasonable to question. Whatever the case, the faculty called Galileo "the Wrangler."

Galileo's behavior was probably a manifestation of his disdain for aspects of the academy. He bristled at his teachers' demeanor: pretentious, arrogant, and uncritically dependent on tradition. In a later satirical poem against academic life, Galileo compared his professors to the Pharisees. Galileo felt that many of the professors clung blindly to tradition despite conflicting reasons or evidence. Not only that, these professors had distorted the tradition. Just as the Pharisees had distorted the law of Moses in their zeal to uphold it, so, too, the professors had distorted Aristotle's method of science. Galileo would later say that if Aristotle were now alive, he would have gladly changed his views on nature—and he would do so on the basis of Aristotelian scientific method. Galileo argued that he was a more faithful disciple of Aristotle than the Aristotelians.

Not surprisingly, Galileo didn't endear himself to the faculty of arts in Pisa. Nor they to him.

≈

In Pisa, Galileo was introduced to mathematics, but not at the university. The introduction would begin a passionate love affair, nonetheless. The matchmaker was Ostilio Ricci, the court mathematician of the grand duke of Tuscany.

Every year around Christmas, the grand duke's court relocated from Florence to Pisa, staying until Easter. Galileo and Ricci met during one of these government sojourns. It is unclear just how they met. Ricci and Vincenzio Galilei were both associated with Tuscan court life, so perhaps Ricci was already friendly with the Galilei family.

Whatever the case, during the winter of 1583, when Galileo was a second-year student, he found Ricci lecturing on Euclid's *Elements* to the court pages. These lectures on geometry were open only to members of the Tuscan court, and so Galileo could not stay to listen.[1] But something about Euclid immediately bewitched him. Unbeknownst to Ricci, Galileo hid behind a door to overhear the lesson. This clandestine practice turned into a habit.[2]

Galileo wasn't the only person enchanted by Euclid's *Elements*. The *Elements* has a long history of seducing great intellects. For most of us who studied geometry in our school days, this effect of Euclid is baffling. To be sure, geometry incites strong feelings, but usually panic and mind-numbing bewilderment—certainly not love at first sight.

But it would be difficult to overstate the *Elements'*—and therefore mathematics'—significance in Western thought. Other than the Bible, Euclid's is the most widely translated book in history. And the reason why is what attracted Galileo.

The *Elements*, or *Stoicheia*—the same Greek term used for the physical elements—is a massive collection of mathematical facts. This, by itself, isn't impressive. What is impressive is the *Elements'* logical structure. This structure charmed Galileo, and it would be partially responsible for his trial. This merely confirms what most of us already suspected. Mathematics is trouble.

$$\approx$$

Nearly all we know about Euclid is that he wrote the *Elements* around 300 BC in Egyptian Alexandria, the Greek cultural successor to ancient Athens. The *Elements* is a mathematical book. It is a book about geometry and therefore about shapes—points, lines, triangles, circles. There is, however, nothing numerical about it. The West's mathematical foundation uses no numbers at all.

The *Elements'* thirteen chapters, or "books," collectively contain 465 geometrical facts—"theorems," we call them (Euclid called them "propositions"). The forty-seventh fact of Book I, for example, is what we now call the Pythagorean theorem, actually first proven in China, long before Pythagoras. These theorems qualify *as theorems* because they are proven by the inviolable laws of logic. They are deduced.

But no one—at least no one finite—can prove everything they believe. The child who repeatedly asks *why* must eventually stop, for Pete's sake. Some things must simply be assumed, taken for granted. These stopping points, these bare assumptions, are called *axioms*. And because axioms aren't argued for, they must have excellent credentials; they must be *obviously* true. A strong building must have a strong foundation.

And here it is, at last, the desirable feature of the *Elements*. If Euclid's assumptions are true and, furthermore, if he carefully adhered to the laws logic, then the theorems—the facts derived—*must* be true. We can, in other words, be certain of our results. And certainty has proven to be a siren song.

But this axiomatic method is even more important than we have suggested. It is not merely the ideal method of mathematics. It was Aristotle's *scientific* method. Science begins, said Aristotle, with indubitable axioms based on observation, on sense experience. From these observational axioms, the natural philosopher then deduces further facts about nature. Science, like mathematics, therefore, was to be a coherent system of knowledge that began with sense experience and grew by way of reason. This standard, we have since discovered, is impossibly high. But in Galileo's time, everyone believed it was possible—even Galileo.

5

"IGNORANCE OF MOTION IS IGNORANCE OF NATURE"

After overhearing Ricci's lectures, Galileo quickly gained his mathematical bearings and began to study Euclid on his own. But he eventually returned to Ricci with questions. And these questions were subtle enough to genuinely impress the old man.[1] When Ricci asked Galileo who was his teacher, he was no doubt amazed to hear that Galileo's only formal mathematical training was a few stolen lectures—Ricci's lectures. What amazes *us* is that mathematics could be a guilty pleasure.

After Easter 1583, the Tuscan court moved back to Florence, and Galileo continued his determined avoidance of every subject other than mathematics (and some philosophy). That summer Galileo met often with Ricci while at home in Florence. Ricci was a frequent visitor to the Galilei household, but Vincenzio was unaware of Ricci's intellectual influence on Galileo. Galileo was not about to tell his father that he had been skipping class in order to study philosophy and mathematics. It's not that Vincenzio was against these disciplines in principle—he was a musician, after all, and music was part of mathematics; rather, Vincenzio didn't want Galileo wasting his time on subjects that weren't going to provide a decent living.

So that summer Galileo continued his secret studies. And whenever he studied his forbidden subjects, he kept a medical text near him. That way, whenever his father suddenly appeared, he could quickly pretend he was diligently studying medicine.[2] Teenagers.

Galileo realized that this act would eventually have to stop, so he spoke with Ricci, who agreed to talk with Vincenzio. Apprised of the situation, Vincenzio knew that Galileo was going to study mathematics and philosophy with or without his permission. Plus, the young man had natural mathematical talent, and so he might as well receive the proper training. Vincenzio permitted Ricci to help Galileo, but Ricci was to pretend that Vincenzio disapproved entirely. Otherwise Galileo would get the wrong idea, namely, that it was okay to neglect his medical studies. Vincenzio knew that he had to compromise, but he didn't have to let Galileo know it. The charade continued.

And so that fall Galileo returned to Pisa and diligently neglected his medical studies.

≈

After Mass at the Cathedral of Pisa one evening, in the shadow of the Leaning Tower, one of the hanging lamps caught Galileo's attention. Maybe an attendant had pulled the lamp close to light it, and when he let it go, the lamp swung away. The lamp's arc, of course, decreased as it swung back and forth. None of this is particularly interesting, other than the swinging fire, but Galileo noticed something curious about the lamp's motion. As the lamp's arc decreased, the amount of time it took the lamp to travel back and forth didn't. The time of oscillation—measured against Galileo's pulse—remained constant regardless the size of the arc.

Countless people had seen an object swinging from the end of a rope or chain, but, for some reason, this Italian college kid was drawn toward a subtle but significant detail. There is seeing, and then there is *seeing*.

Galileo's discovery of the pendulum's isochronous behavior would be used a few years later to develop (ironically) a medical device to measure a patient's pulse—the *pulsilogium*.[3] And as an old man, under house arrest, Galileo would use the principle to invent a pendulum clock. But the importance of this event far transcends the pendulum's significance. For the first time, Galileo turned his attention to motion itself, where time mysteriously mingles with distance.

≈

Motion is ubiquitous in nature. Even the very earth moves, although no one knew it at the time, and only a handful had even guessed it.

To Aristotle, and therefore to Europe, motion was the most fundamental topic in natural philosophy. The scholastics had pithily reformulated a famous passage in Aristotle's *Physics*:[4] "Ignorance of motion is ignorance of nature." In fact, Aristotle defined nature—that is, physics—as the "principle of motion and change."[5] Nature *is* motion.

Aristotle believed that in order to have genuine knowledge in physics—to understand motion—we must know what causes motion, what explains it. We may be able to *describe* a particular instance of motion in detail, but this is not an explanation. A description, by itself, is a *how* without a *why*.

Consider an example. When an apple comes loose from its tree, it moves toward the center of the earth. This—admittedly, not much—is a description of the event. But it doesn't say why the apple moves like that. This isn't because it's a bad description; it's just not an explanation. (According to Aristotle's physics, the apple's earthy nature causes it to fall toward the center of the cosmos.)

And because the goal of Aristotelian science is to discover the cause of motion, Aristotle did not incorporate mathematics. Mathematics—as Aristotle well knew (and modern physicists often forget)—does not say what causes objects to behave the way they do. It only describes how they behave.

Aristotle's study of nature, then, was qualitative rather than quantitative. That is, he used terms like *faster*, *slower*, *heavier*, and *lighter*, but he assigned no numbers to objects or their properties. And though Aristotle's physics lacked precise and powerful mathematical descriptions, he made up for it by providing fundamental causal explanations. This was his strength and weakness. But it would not be Galileo's. Galileo would eventually abandon the search for fundamental physical causes; his new goal would be mathematical descriptions. This would be part of the scientific coup against Aristotle.

6

A WORLD OF MACHINES

lthough Galileo attended Mass, he didn't extend that honor to his medical classes. By the middle of Galileo's third year, in early 1584, the university notified Vincenzio that his son was in danger of failing. Vincenzio took this as an opportunity to visit Tedaldi in Pisa and check on his son. Tedaldi, however, assured Vincenzio that Galileo was incessantly studying.[1] Just not medicine.

It was time for the pretense to stop. Vincenzio confronted Galileo, who confessed to having no interest whatsoever in medicine. Vincenzio threatened to remove all financial support unless Galileo promised to set aside these distractions and finish medical school.[2] Galileo refused, but asked his father to be patient, to support him one more year. After that, he promised, he would take care of himself.[3]

It was clear to Vincenzio that Galileo wasn't lazy. Perhaps, given his remarkable intelligence, he could even find success in mathematics. And it would be better to help his son in this case than to risk alienating him. Vincenzio, therefore, agreed to finance Galileo's education one more year.

By the end of his fourth year, Galileo was in a position to take a degree (probably in philosophy).[4] Yet he didn't, and we don't know why. In the spring of 1585, Galileo returned to Florence a college dropout. He was twenty-one and unemployed. And to make matters worse, his parents' home was already overcrowded. Galileo needed to pull his weight.

≈

At this point, Galileo's story could go well or not. The world has seen many intelligent young men who simply couldn't get their acts together. There has been no shortage of frustrated parents and teachers who have tried in vain to *get that kid going*.

But Galileo was not one to go slack. He immediately began looking for teaching posts in Italian universities. While searching, he offered private instruction in mathematics and philosophy. During this time Ricci introduced Galileo to another of his ancient acquaintances: Archimedes. And this time it was on purpose. Whereas Euclid had provided Galileo with a mathematical method, Archimedes put that method to use to describe nature. This may have been just what Galileo had been looking for; at any rate, it was just what he needed.

Applying mathematics to the physical world wasn't new, even to Archimedes. The ancient Greeks—and the Egyptians and Babylonians before them—had long used geometry to describe the heavens. But Archimedes applied Euclid's geometry to the unruly terrestrial realm, and this *was* new. And because

Archimedes's works were lost until the Renaissance, it was new in Galileo's time too.

Of course, by applying the *Elements* to physics, Archimedes rejected Aristotle's goal of finding physical causes. Archimedes apparently felt that the gain in mathematical precision made mere description worthwhile. As we alluded to earlier, Galileo agreed.

Archimedes, however, did not describe *moving* objects, only those that conveniently stood still. And even though astronomers had mathematically mapped the positions of objects like the sun, moon, and stars, these heavenly bodies moved slowly enough to consider their motion as discreet snapshots of stationary positions. Galileo, on the other hand, wished to apply mathematics to both stationary *and* moving objects. He could rely on Archimedes' example for the former but found only hints for the latter.

What Galileo had in mind—using mathematics to describe motion—bordered on impossible. We do it today with such aplomb that we have forgotten that it's magical. Just *why* mathematics works is a great mystery—unless, of course, there is a divine Designer. Galileo remarked that the very fact that humans can discover facts about nature through mathematical proofs proves that "the human mind is a work of God and one of the most excellent."[5]

Galileo would remain an avowed student of Archimedes his entire life. He gushed over Archimedes' discoveries, exclaiming that anyone who has "read and understood the very subtle inventions of this divine man in his own writings . . . most clearly realizes how inferior all other minds are to Archimedes's and what small hope is left to anyone of ever discovering things similar to his."[6]

≈

One of the most famous stories in the history of science involves a soaking wet, naked man. Overjoyed at a discovery made while bathing, Archimedes raced through the streets of Syracuse, naked, shouting, "Eureka! Eureka!" or, "I found it!"

Of course, the memorable part of the legend isn't its most significant. While relaxing in the public baths of Syracuse, Archimedes discovered the hydrostatic principle, a principle now bearing his name. It is a dull principle that, in itself, has very limited application. But the mechanism upon which it is founded would change our metaphor of the universe.

To understand Archimedes' principle, imagine throwing a plastic gallon jug filled with mustard into a swimming pool. Will the jug of mustard float? Archimedes discovered that the answer depends on whether a gallon of mustard weighs more than a gallon of water (to make things simpler, ignore the weight of the jug). If a gallon of mustard weighs more than a gallon of pool water, then it will sink; if not, it will float. And this is true for any object thrown into water, whether an ice cube or a cat.

Here's the important part: Archimedes analyzed floating bodies in terms of a scale or balance. That is, he imagined that the gallon of mustard was placed on one side of a scale, the gallon of water on the other. To see the physical situation this way requires a perspective that in many contexts would count as insanity. We often scoff at geniuses because their ideas seem simply mad.

This picture of a balance suggested one of the most fertile metaphors of nature, even if not the most obvious. Fundamentally, a balance is a lever, and a lever is a simple machine, a man-made device for doing work. Archimedes is famous for saying that if he had a place to stand and a lever long enough, he could move the earth.[7] Archimedes' pithy saying was prophetic; Galileo would be its fulfillment.

Moreover, the concept of the simple machine—in particular, the lever or balance—would become, for Galileo, the very idea of what it means for nature to be intelligible.[8] This would be perhaps the biggest conceptual departure from Aristotle. As we saw, the prevailing metaphor for the Aristotelian universe was that of a biological organism. This metaphor provided a powerful conceptual framework, eyeglasses through which to see the world. But Galileo would prescribe a new set of lenses. From here on, science's reigning metaphor would be an inert and lifeless machine, but one intelligently *designed*.

The metaphor of a machine brought with it optimism not provided by the old organism metaphor. A machine is far less complex than a living thing, and therefore easier to understand. Furthermore, simple machines like the lever are much more amenable to mathematics. In accepting the mechanical world picture, therefore, scientists began to *believe*; they became confident that they could discover nature's deepest secrets. And, as in sports, confidence can separate success from defeat.

The mechanical metaphor would begin to seep into the rest of society. With bookkeeping's balanced accounts and international commerce's balance of trade, Archimedes' model of mechanical equilibrium was a prolific picture.[9] And although we normally associate the mechanical worldview with a clock, it was the balance—through Galileo—that did the bulk of the conceptual work.[10] And even the clock was a form of pendulum, which itself could be modeled as a balance.[11]

In 1586, Galileo wrote his first complete scientific treatise—*La Bilancetta* or *The Little Balance*. In it, he described a new type of hydrostatic balance, one that operated on Archimedes's principle. A year later Galileo made advancements in calculating centers of gravity, an Archimedian subject that also depended on balance or equilibrium. Galileo was beginning to put science—and therefore nature—in the balance.

7

THE GEOMETRY
OF HELL

Galileo no doubt found his Archimedian work stimulating and edifying, but he still needed a job. Money was important, of course, but at this point it wasn't the main consideration. He desired an academic career, particularly in mathematics. But such teaching posts were rare, and vacant ones rarer still, vacated by resignation or death.

Even if a chair in mathematics was vacated—or a new one created—there would be stiff competition. And competition would be a problem for Galileo at this point. In 1587 he was only twenty-three, unemployed, and still unpublished; *The Little Balance* and his work on centers of gravity were merely manuscripts. Furthermore, Galileo needed recommendations, and his professional contacts were scanty. Ricci, of course, could vouch for Galileo's mathematical abilities, but despite Ricci's impressive background, he was an academic outsider, a court mathematician and practical engineer. And Galileo certainly couldn't count on his professors at Pisa: they would no doubt say the wrong sorts of things to a potential employer. That bridge lay in cinders.

This was Galileo's personal political situation at the time he learned of an opening at the University of Bologna.[1] The mathematics chair had been vacated, albeit involuntarily—its former occupant had died.[2] Since Bologna was officially under control of the papacy, an obvious place for Galileo to seek recommendations was in Rome. So in the fall of 1587, Galileo made his first trip to the Eternal City.[3]

$$\approx$$

The Society of Jesus was founded in 1540 as an educational and proselytizing monastic order.[4] The Jesuits, as its members were called, were the "real sword" of the sixteenth-century Counter-Reformation.[5] Part of why they were effective was that they had become the "chief teachers of Europe."[6] By 1580, the Jesuits had founded 140 colleges, their principal college being the Collegio Romano in Rome.[7]

In the 1580s, the Society established a general curriculum, the *Ratio Studiorum* (Method of Study), as a guide for Jesuit colleges.[8] Not surprisingly, much of the curriculum covered theology and moral philosophy. But the *Ratio* also placed considerable emphasis on natural philosophy. The Jesuits, in fact, had devoted more resources to studying the natural world than perhaps anyone up to that time.

The *Ratio* also elevated the study of mathematics to an unprecedented level.[9] This emphasis was due to the influence of one of the *Ratio*'s main authors, the leading Jesuit mathematician Christopher Clavius, from Germany.[10] Clavius was the finest mathematician in Europe and hailed as the "Euclid of the Sixteenth Century."[11] And now Galileo hoped that some of Clavius's reputation would rub off.

It was a genuine honor for a young, unemployed mathematician to meet the great Clavius, but Father Clavius treated Galileo graciously. Galileo had brought with him his work on centers of gravity, and Clavius was impressed—Galileo had indeed gone beyond Archimedes.[12] Unfortunately, we have no record of Clavius's recommendation to the University of Bologna on Galileo's behalf. But being in the good graces of the Jesuits was more than worth the trip.

Disappointingly, the mathematics position at Bologna was given to Giovanni Magini, an astronomer from Padua. Magini was older and more experienced, having already published a number of books.[13] This was not the last time that Magini and Galileo would compete for a chair in mathematics. It would, however, be the last time Galileo lost.

〜

While Galileo was garnering support in Rome, Francesco de Medici, Duke of Tuscany, died unexpectedly at the age of forty-two (quite young, as most forty-two-year-olds will point out).[14] Francesco's wife, the lovely Venetian Bianca Capello, died less than twelve hours later. This was, of course, odd. Odder still was that Francesco's estranged brother, Ferdinando—a cardinal since he was sixteen—was in town for an overdue visit. Cardinal

Ferdinando had disapproved of Bianca because she had been Francesco's mistress before she was his wife. To remove any doubt about his innocence, Ferdinando ordered an autopsy and, despite rumors to the contrary, it seems he had nothing to do with their deaths.[15]

Francesco, however, had no sons, and so Ferdinando was elected grand duke of Tuscany. He resigned his cardinalate and asked for permission to marry Christina of Lorraine, an unflinchingly devout Catholic.[16] Christina was intelligent and well educated—her aunt, Catherine de Medici, the queen of France, had made sure of that.[17]

Ferdinando's marriage to Christina was the occasion of a great Florentine party. Normally, Galileo's father, Vincenzio, would have prepared the wedding music. But he wasn't even invited to the wedding. It seems that he had fallen out of favor with the new duke. Vincenzio had been fond of Bianca, dedicating a book of music to her, and he therefore inherited some of Ferdinando's disapproval. Vincenzio, however, wasn't expelled from the Tuscan court; he was simply ignored.

≈

Dante Alighieri—*the* Dante—was a Florentine treasure. His great poem *The Divine Comedy* (1300) is a convenient dividing line between the Middle Ages and the Renaissance, even if in reality the line is a century-wide blur. Dante's epic poem is influential, in part, because of the cosmos it presented to Europe. Very few things transform imaginations like a great story—other than perhaps a great story told using great poetry. Such stories change men and therefore the world. Philosophy can only do so much by itself; combine it with literature and watch it take hold.

In *The Divine Comedy*, Dante travels through a modified Aristotelian cosmos, one adapted to the teachings of the Church and Scripture.[18] (Dante had called Aristotle "the Master of those who know."[19]) Outside the universe is God's throne; at the cosmos's center is the earth. Below the earth's surface, farthest away from the divine dwelling, is hell. And separating man from God were the celestial spheres, the crystalline orbs of the wandering and fixed stars. Angelic beings were responsible for the motion of the heavens and so became part of the astronomical theory. Man occupied an intermediate place between the spiritual and the material, just as each individual human did, being made of body and soul. In *The Divine Comedy*, the "vastest of all themes, the theme of human sin and salvation, is adjusted to the great plan of the universe."[20] And once Dante fixed this plan in the European imagination, moving the earth implied that we move God's throne.[21]

In the intervening centuries, Italian scholars, especially Florentine scholars, had pored over Dante's work. They had analyzed it, interpreted it, and reveled in it. They took literary criticism so seriously that they debated the exact dimensions of Dante's cone-shaped hell.

This hellish problem had proved recalcitrant to scholars of a literary and philosophical bent. In 1588, the famous Platonic Florentine Academy (not the University of Florence, which was all but defunct) decided to consult someone who had more breadth, someone familiar with mathematics as well as literature and philosophy. This made good sense; after all, mathematics and hell are close allies.

It was probably Ricci—himself a member of the Florentine Academy—who proposed that Galileo be chosen. The Academy agreed, and so Galileo presented his *Two Lectures to the Florentine Academy on the Shape, Place, and Size of Dante's Inferno*. Not surprisingly, Galileo enlisted Archimedes' assistance. "We shall," Galileo began, "reckon according to the things demonstrated by Archimedes in his books *On the Sphere* and *On the Cylinder*."[22] Galileo went on to argue that, given what Dante says, Lucifer's height is 1,935 arm lengths.[23] The Academy was delighted.

Galileo agreed with Dante that God had put the earth at the center of the cosmos to "have it as far as possible from the sight of the blessed residents of Heaven lest they be offended by its grossness."[24] This belied the common claim that the eventual relocation of the earth from the center of the universe would be a religious affront; rather than demoting man from his place of central position, it moved him farther away from hell. Again, when it comes to the story of Galileo, the devil is in the details—and he may not always like what they imply.

≈

Galileo's name was becoming known. Although his work on centers of gravity did not win him the Bolognese post, it did win him his first acclaim outside of Italy. In 1588, the Italian geographer Abraham Ortelius sent a copy to an important Belgian mathematician, Michael Coignet.[25] Coignet wrote Galileo to express his admiration, commenting that the theorems would be of great practical value. And in Italy, the treatise was praised by Giuseppe Moletti, a mathematics professor at the prestigious University of Padua.[26]

But most important of all, Galileo sent a copy of his theorems to the Marquis Guidobaldo del Monte, who had just written what would become the sixteenth century's most important work on terrestrial physics.[27] Del Monte's respect for the twenty-four-year-old Galileo was evident; del Monte sent his own book on Archimedes to Galileo, saying that "he would value Galileo's opinion more than anyone else's."[28] Their friendship—and del Monte's patronage—would last until del Monte's death eighteen years later.[29] And it didn't hurt that the Marquis had connections, including his brother Francesco, who lived in Florence. Francesco had the grand duke's ear.[30]

There was finally an opening at the University of Pisa: the mathematics professor, Filippo Fantoni, resigned to become head of his Camaldolese order. Galileo applied for the position with the recommendation of del Monte and del Monte's brother, Francesco.[31] Unfortunately, Fantoni soon returned to his teaching post at Pisa.

Galileo had no other prospects. Just as Galileo's father had feared—and no doubt had warned—it was going to be very difficult to secure a mathematics position. Had Galileo stayed with medicine, he would already be establishing his career. But now was probably not the time to mention that.

8

TORTURING NATURE

One reason Galileo would be hailed as the originator of modern physics is that he extended Archimedes' use of geometry to the study of motion. Another reason, however, is that Galileo also extended the use of observation. Recall that Aristotle's science was founded upon observation. Statements describing these observations would become the axioms of science, its foundation. *Observing* is simply a matter of looking at what occurs naturally in the world, and this is something quite different from *experimenting*. Experimenting is *intervening*, artificially manipulating the world to make it perform. The English philosopher Francis Bacon called it "putting nature to the test," a euphemism for torture (although, oddly, Bacon used this phrase approvingly).

For Aristotle, however, experimenting was going too far. Intervening in the physical world's ordinary operations would interfere with the very natures or essences in which scientists are interested. That is, after all, why science was called *natural* philosophy.

Galileo would be a bridge connecting observation and experiment, despite the fact that he didn't always use experiments the way we think he should have. In fact, Galileo would downplay experiments far more than is commonly attributed to him. Yet a bridge, although not the final destination, is necessary for reaching it.

Again, Archimedes had blazed something of a trail. Because Archimedes had used mathematics in his physical science, he needed at least a minimal type of experiment. The mathematical descriptions needed to be checked. To check them, therefore, Archimedes had to make *measurements*, measurements of objects in the actual world. But he couldn't just stand around all day waiting, like a bird watcher, for nature to show up and do what he wanted it to. He had to be proactive.

It might seem, therefore, that Galileo learned to value experiments from Archimedes. But it is more likely that he learned it from his father, Vincenzio. A few years earlier, Vincenzio had been involved in a controversy that centered on the relative authority of mathematics and sense experience. In his 1581 book *Dialogue on Ancient and Modern Music*, he argued against a particular Pythagorean view of music theory that was based purely on mathematics. Vincenzio claimed—against his former master Zorlino—that we should *look and see* (or in this case *listen*) whether the Pythagoreans were right about music. (This is the context of the passage discussed earlier in the preface.) Vincenzio said the Pythagoreans were wrong; the mathematics didn't match experience.

In 1588, Vincenzio was embroiled in another similar controversy with Zorlino. Again, the issue was the accuracy of the purely mathematical results of ancient music theory. Vincenzio argued that in certain respects the ancient theory was wrong and adhering to it limited the actual practice of musicians. There are mathematical ratios that sound consonant even though they don't agree with the accepted theory. On paper, they shouldn't be pleasing, but, Vincenzio said, the real test is the musician's ear.

To support his view, Vincenzio performed a series of experiments using strings under varying tension. The experimental setup involved hanging different-sized weights from a string—a pendulum.[1] Galileo, who lived at home during this time, most likely assisted his father. Pendulums would provide an important way for Galileo to test his theory of falling bodies, and so would become a key device in the scientific revolution. At any rate, as it turned out, Vincenzio was right. But if Zorlino had won the argument, Bach would never have written his "Well-Tempered Clavier."[2] This, apparently, would be bad.

Vincenzio wasn't choosing experiment over mathematics. Mathematics and experiments were working together in a system of checks and balances. When they agreed—when they *balanced*—Vincenzio saw this as reasonable evidence that the mathematics was correct and that the experiments had been performed correctly.

Vincenzio was now nearly seventy years old, and his relationship with Galileo had grown deep and affectionate. Perhaps Vincenzio had mellowed with age; or maybe Galileo had matured. No doubt each thought the other had changed.

During their relationship's twilight, Galileo would often accompany his father on the lute or organ. Years later, when Galileo was isolated and entirely blind, his lute would be one of his few sources of solace. Perhaps it reminded him of his father.

9

IN THE SHADOW OF THE LEANING TOWER

I n 1589, Galileo had been out of college for four years, and there were still no prospects for a teaching post. Although he was loath to leave Florence, he resigned himself to look for a position, not merely outside of Italy, but in the Middle East.

In the eleventh hour, however, Fillipo Fantoni, the vacillating mathematics professor at Pisa, stepped down again. On the strength of new references—including those of del Monte and Grand Duke Ferdinando—Galileo was hired. It was his first official job. He was twenty-five.

Galileo signed a three-year renewable contract. Unfortunately, it paid very little. For one thing, Pisa was no Jesuit college, so, as in most universities, mathematics was considered a minor discipline. For another thing, Galileo was an unproven commodity—young, no previous professorship, and no publications. The university paid Fantoni twice the amount offered Galileo, but he had held the chair for years.

In the fall the Arno River flooded, delaying Galileo's arrival in Pisa. The university consequently fined him for missing his first six lectures. The following summer he was fined again, this time for an eighteen-day absence during which he was in Florence, taking care of his critically ill mother.[1] His small salary was becoming smaller still. At least he was a bachelor, though, and had relatively few expenses.

The Pisan professors no doubt remembered the Wrangler, and relations didn't improve even with Galileo on this side of the lectern. And neither did Galileo's attitude toward academic pretension. Galileo wrote a three-hundred-line poem—*Against the Donning of the Gown*—satirizing academic ritual. At places the poem was crude, highlighting Galileo's disdain for academic protocol. Galileo joked, for example, that the gowns would prevent men and women's frank appraisals of one another.[2] Although Galileo meant the poem only for his friends,[3] it was circulated nonetheless, winning him few friends among the faculty.

Despite his lack of popularity with many of the philosophy professors, Galileo made a few very close friends at Pisa. One of them was even a philosopher—Jacobo Mazzoni. Years earlier, Mazzoni had won a memory contest by reciting an unbelievable 5,193 proverbs or maxims.[4]

Galileo and Mazzoni had many spirited disagreements over philosophy, which Galileo wistfully recalled in a letter when he was older.[5] He enjoyed few things more than discussing a controversial issue with friends over a bottle of wine.

~

At Pisa, Galileo wrote a treatise called *De Motu* or *On Motion*, a topic he had studied while unemployed in Florence. The Aristotelian science of motion—as we saw—was a philosopher's discipline, not a mathematician's; it was the study of physical causes, not mathematical descriptions. Yet in the *De Motu*, Galileo attempted to combine both. Of this new application of mathematics to motion, Galileo said:

> In this treatise the method we shall follow will be always to make what is said depend on what is said before, and never, if possible, to assume as true that which requires proof. My teachers of mathematics taught me that.[6]

Galileo was clear about his methodological goal. "He would apply mathematics to the real world and replace the wordy fumblings of the philosophers with true knowledge."[7] Despite this methodological change, the *De Motu*'s content was largely Aristotelian.

But there was one issue on which Aristotle and Galileo disagreed. Aristotle had said that the speed of falling bodies depends on their weight or "heaviness" (*gravitas*), and so heavier objects fall faster than lighter ones. Galileo, on the other hand, believed that any two objects, regardless of weight, would fall at the same speed. A bullet and a cannonball dropped simultaneously from the same height would reach the ground together. Their weight is irrelevant, unless they landed on your toes.

To convince the Aristotelians, Galileo, according to legend, dropped different-sized objects from Pisa's leaning campanile. Viviani is the source of this legend, but many scholars question his story because he was caught exaggerating others. Yet Drake argues that we have good reasons for believing the story and that most of the doubts are derived from embellishments made to Viviani's story, not from the Viviani's original telling.[8]

In any case, such an experiment would make it easy to determine who was right. According to Aristotle's physics, a hundred-pound iron ball should fall ten times as fast as a ten-pound iron ball. Galileo, on the other hand, claimed that the balls would fall at the same speed.

Unfortunately, neither of the results occurred. Galileo later wrote to an Aristotelian:

> You find, on making the test, that the larger ball beats the smaller one by two inches. Now, behind those two inches you want to hide Aristotle's ninety-nine cubits and, speaking only of my tiny error, remain silent about his enormous mistake.[9]

The philosophers apparently would not budge. The two inches were caused by the air's resistance; the Aristotelians' resistance was due to their master's authority.

Galileo knew why his experiment hadn't gone exactly as planned. He realized—even then—that there's a difference between the real world and the ideal world described by mathematics. Even Archimedes' law of the lever applies only to imaginary levers that are perfectly straight, rigid, and massless.[10]

We should ignore, said Galileo, things like the resistance of the air, what he called the "material hindrances." We should also ignore the object's shape, size, and color. This dramatically simplifies the situation, while easing the application of mathematics. We of course have to know what can be legitimately ignored, and for this, there is no hard-and-fast rule. It takes an intuition that very few people had in Galileo's time. We only know now because we have been taught.

What is troubling is that these simplified and idealized scenarios aren't *real*. And in cases where they are (e.g., out in space) they aren't *idealized*. Idealization and simplification are strange methods for those in the business of discovering what the world is *actually* like. The Catholic philosopher of science Ernan McMullin explains that idealization will eventually define the domain of science. Science will search for the reality "actually happening behind the forbiddingly complex appearances in which the mathematically exact structures of the real are cloaked."[11] On this view, a phenomenon like friction just gets in the way of reality.

But what reasons are there to suppose that the idealized world is the real world? Not many, but one reason is a belief that reality is fundamentally mathematical. This is the ancient faith of Pythagoras, and we are, it seems, part of the Pythagorean brotherhood. Just like Galileo.

⚊

In the summer of 1591, Vincenzio died at the age of seventy. Galileo had his father's body placed in the Basilica in Santa Croce "in accordance with ancestral tradition."[12] Being the oldest son, Galileo now bore the financial burden of his family's well-being. Three of his siblings had died in childhood, but there were still his mother, his two sisters (Virginia and Livia), and his sixteen-year-old brother, Michelangelo. Galileo's meager salary was barely enough for a single young man with no family responsibilities. For much of his adult life, Galileo would be strapped for money.

Yet for now, he managed, probably by increasing the number of students he tutored. Whatever the case, he was able to continue paying for Livia to remain at the Convent of San Giuliano until he could ensure her a suitable marriage. Virginia was soon to be married to Benedetto Landucci, and it fell upon Galileo to pay her dowry installments.

Galileo was apparently an attentive brother. Just before Virginia's wedding, Galileo wrote to his mother, Giulia:

> The present I am going to make Virginia consists of a set of silken bed-hangings . . . I bought the silk at Lucca, and had it woven, so that, though the fabric is of a wide width, it will cost me only about three carlini the yard. It is a striped material, and I think you will be much pleased with it. I have ordered silk fringes to match, and could very easily get the bedstead made, too. But do not say a word to anyone, that it may come to her quite unexpectedly. I will bring it when I come home for the Carnival holidays, and, as I said before, if you like I will bring her worked velvet and damask, stuff enough to make four or five handsome dresses.[13]

This passage seems calculated to delight—the supposedly hard-nosed and combative scientist, tending to the dainties of silken bedclothes, excited with the anticipation of a surprise.

But within a year or two, Galileo fell behind on his dowry installments. And once—when he was about to return to Florence for summer vacation—his mother warned:

> Come, but you should know that Benedetto wants his money now and is threatening to have you forcibly arrested immediately when you arrive here . . . He is just the man to do it, so I warn you: it would grieve me much if anything of the kind were to happen.[14]

Galileo went to Florence anyway and borrowed the money. Benedetto himself cosigned the loan.[15]

In 1592, Galileo's tenure at the University of Pisa was nearing its end. With the rancor he had stirred up among the Pisan faculty, he was almost certain that the university would not renew his contract. Nor did he exactly want it to. (At least he and the other professors could agree on this.) His friends, furthermore, wanted him at a university whose prestige was more commensurate with his great, albeit emerging, talent. And that wasn't at Pisa.

10

PADUAN PLEASANTNESS

The Serene Republic of Venice controlled Padua and was extremely proud of the city's university—faculty appointments were matters of state. The University of Padua may have been the most prestigious in Europe.[1] It had excellent professors, well-stocked libraries, and healthy financial support from the Venetian Senate.[2]

Venice was the only completely independent state in Italy, managing to keep Rome out of its political affairs. This relative political freedom also made the University of Padua a safe haven for Protestant scholars. Compared to other Italian universities, the University of Padua had an air of intellectual freedom that made it relatively vibrant. But the atmosphere was ambivalent. Sometimes the freedom could be dangerous, giving overly exuberant professors just enough rope with which to hang themselves.

The University of Padua's mathematics chair had been vacant since the great Giuseppe Moletti died in 1588. But officials were waiting for just the right person, someone who could fill Moletti's giant shoes. Giovanni Magini, Galileo's rival at Bologna, had no doubt applied for the position—Padua was Magini's hometown. But Galileo's reputation as a mathematician had grown since their first showdown.

Galileo visited Padua in the fall of 1592, and the university was impressed by what it saw. Moreover, Galileo's advocates—especially del Monte and the head of the Florentine Academy—had provided stellar recommendations. So, despite still having published nothing, Galileo won the coveted mathematics chair, forcing Magini to remain in Bologna. Galileo, being a Tuscan—a foreigner—needed permission from the grand duke to take the post. The duke approved, and Galileo was appointed for six years, at triple his Pisan pay. He would remain in Padua for eighteen years—years he would later describe as the happiest of his life.

The main pastime of Paduan intellectuals was gathering at homes for dinner and conversation. In this way, professors and nonacademics mingled, increasing the interplay of academics, religion, and politics. One of the main meeting places was the home of Gian Vincenzo Pinelli. Pinelli received dignitaries from abroad and had an enviable library of books and manuscripts.[3] Unfortunately, much of his library was later lost at sea.[4]

The young Galileo was fortunate to find lodging with Pinelli. Living with Pinelli, Galileo made important contacts that would later change his life. The two most important were the Servite friar Paolo Sarpi and the Jesuit cardinal Robert Bellarmine, the two of whom would later lock horns in a standoff between Venice and Rome.

Padua fit Galileo's personality. He loved to argue, and his fiery temperament matched his reddish hair; Vivani says he was quick to anger but just as quickly mollified.[5] Moreover, Galileo "was of average stature, squarely built, and of lively appearance and disposition."

> His unusual talents as a speaker and as a teacher are beyond question. Among those who knew him personally, even including adversaries, few seem to have disliked him . . . Pugnacious rather than belligerent, he refrained from starting polemic battles but was ruthless in their prosecution when he answered an attack at all . . . His friends included artists and men of letters as well as mathematicians and scientists; cardinals as well as rulers; craftsmen as well as learned men. His enemies included conservative professors, several priests, most philosophers, and those scientists who had publicly challenged him and felt the bite of his sarcasm in return.[6]

Galileo was not the typical scientist, which is exactly why we remember him. Ernan McMullin explains that

> most of his life was spent not in observing, not in calculating, not in proving, but simply in persuading . . . His historic role was to change a world view, and this demanded talents of a far more diverse order than would be required by the simple establishment of a new theory.[7]

Galileo kept extremely busy between his involvement in Padua's intellectual scene, his university responsibilities, and his own research. He also tutored to supplement his income. Even though his salary was larger, it was not intended to be a living wage, and supplemental teaching was expected.[8] This reveals how meager his Pisan pay was.

~

Padua was famous for its medical program. There was a strong experimental program in the medical school, which included a small theatre in which the famous physician and anatomist, Fabrizio di Acquapendente, performed autopsies.[9] Fabrizio also became Galileo's private physician, something Galileo would frequently need.

But as renowned as its medical curriculum was, Padua was just as famous for housing the most sophisticated school of Aristotelianism. Cesare Cremonini sat in the philosophy chair and was one of Europe's ablest advocates of Aristotle's philosophy. Cremonini and Galileo became instant and close friends, their heated but friendly discussions a common occurrence at Pinelli's house.

Galileo gave his inaugural lecture on December 7, 1592. As professor of mathematics, his courses included Euclid's *Elements* (especially book V on proportions) and Ptolemy's astronomy. Even the medical students were required to study astronomy in order to cast reliable horoscopes. To us, horoscopes are silly. But at the time, astrology was part of astronomy, and astronomers—Catholics and Protestants alike—generally cast horoscopes. Even today, physicists tell us that heavenly objects play a part in earthly events, mysteriously tugging and pulling at us across empty space without any physical contact. What could be "sillier"?

A course in astronomy was actually a course in mathematics, not natural philosophy. Early in Western history a division of labor had occurred in the celestial disciplines. This division resulted in two confused traditions—astronomy and cosmology. Renaissance astronomy was Ptolemy's; Renaissance cosmology, Aristotle's. Both were *geocentric*, or "earth centered," and Galileo was beginning to believe neither of them.

EARTH DISPLACED

Aristotle's beloved teacher, Plato, had arrived at the idea of a spherical universe on aesthetic grounds—a spherical universe was philosophically pleasing. After all, the Greeks believed, the sphere is the perfect shape. The spherical universe, with the earth at the center, also accounted for most of the celestial motions. Most. The wandering stars—the planets—were a problem. They sped up, slowed down, and sometimes reversed direction. All in all, they misbehaved.

But Plato was a Pythagorean and so believed that even the planets' impropriety was orderly and mathematical. It is not at all obvious, however, that heavenly motion should have anything to do with mathematics. Imagine watching a drunken man staggering down a street and then being asked to map his motion using only a complex combination of circles. This is essentially the homework problem Plato gave the mathematicians of his Academy in Athens—to mathematically describe the heavenly motions using nothing more than uniformly rotating spheres.

Plato's pupil Eudoxus was the first to turn in his homework, and his spherical model matched the actual motion better than it had a right to.

Neither Plato nor Eudoxus believed that these spheres actually exist. Eudoxus's spherical model was just a handy mathematical tool. The actual physical structure of the cosmos was anybody's guess. The mathematics only described the appearances, or as Plato famously put it, "saved the phenomena."

Aristotle, however, turned these mathematical devices into physical spheres, spheres made out of crystalline aether or quintessence, as we saw. And so for Aristotle, the spheres *caused* the heavens to move as they did. It was a complete system—it mathematically described *and* physically explained. Nice.

But as astronomical observations became more accurate, discrepancies between the mathematics and the observations increased. The Eudoxian/Aristotelian model couldn't match the real motion of the heavens. Astronomers—the mathematicians—worked furiously to make the mathematics fit the observed data. They added more circles and offset the centers of others. By the second century AD, Ptolemy, the great ancient Alexandrian astronomer, had added circles whose centers traveled around the center of other circles. Circles circling circles circling circles. In the 1200s, when King Alfonso the Wise of Spain (d. 1284) was introduced to the Ptolemaic system, he reportedly said, "Had I been present at the creation, I would have suggested something simpler."

The entire mathematical system was becoming so cumbersome that there was no way to believe that the mathematical description of the cosmos was its actual structure. Some of the circles, for example, intersected each other, something crystalline spheres simply could not do. The mathematical tool was becoming a mess, while the philosophical theory remained nice and neat. There were now two separate systems, one obviously fictional, the other obviously true. But it is difficult to see why the two would come apart like this, and the schizophrenia became a nagging concern.

In any event, the people who wished to mathematically describe the motion of the heavens—the astronomers—were housed in the mathematics departments of universities. Folks interested in the actual structure of the universe joined the philosophy department, where they studied cosmology.

And so it was in Galileo's time. At Padua, Galileo taught astronomy while his philosopher friend Cremonini stuck to cosmology.

$\approx$

By the 1500s, the astronomical (mathematical) system simply could not keep up with the improved observations. It became impossible to describe the motion of the heavens beyond a rough approximation. This actually had religious ramifications. Calendars were important for predicting holy days, particularly Easter. The Church called for reform, and they called for a Catholic cleric to help.

Nicolaus Copernicus was a church official from Poland who studied astronomy and law at Bologna and Padua. When asked to help reform the calendar, he replied that it would be better to reform astronomy first, to improve the mathematics. Copernicus had no new observations, but he thought there must be a simpler way to mathematically describe the swirling heavens.

But why think that the world should be simple? This is perhaps one of the central questions in science. Why do we think that simpler theories—other things being equal—are closer to the truth? It is nothing more or less than a philosophical preference. And it may be true. Who can say?

While studying in Italy, Copernicus had become familiar with a resuscitated strain of philosophy based on Plato's Pythagoreanism, called *Neoplatonism* ("new platonism"). Both Plato and Pythagoras had stressed the significance and majesty of the sun. Taking cues from Neoplatonism, Copernicus put the sun at the center of the cosmos.

And it worked. Relocating the sun made the mathematics simpler, even if not simple. Copernicus reduced the number of spheres from roughly eighty to thirty. And this simplification is all it had going for it—it failed to describe the motions any more accurately. But it was simple and appealed to a Platonist aesthetic sense. Moreover, Copernicus believed that the sun is actually at the center of the cosmos—he intended his system to be more than a mere mathematical tool.

Almost no one followed him in this. Copernicus went public with his system in 1543, in his *On the Revolution of the Heavenly Spheres*, usually referred to as *De Revolutionibus*. The word *revolution* in the title refers to the circling of the crystalline spheres; it has nothing to do with overthrowing an old regime.

It is, therefore, a delightful and satisfying coincidence that this book began the slow coup that would dethrone Aristotle.

Nevertheless, except for a handful of mathematicians, the book was instantly ignored. Copernicus's rearrangement of the cosmic furniture was seen merely as a calculational device, a work of astronomy rather than cosmology. The preface itself had encouraged this interpretation. Copernicus, however, wasn't the preface's author; the Protestant theologian Andreas Osiander was. Osiander had been put in charge of the *De Revolutionibus*'s publication, and he was worried that Copernicus would be severely attacked by the Aristotelians and theologians if they thought heliocentricity (the *sun-centered* theory) was intended to be taken as a physical theory.

But Copernicus had other things to worry about; he had just suffered from what was probably a stroke. It is said that the first printed copy of the *De Revolutionibus* was placed in his dying hands. He apparently never knew of the misleading preface.

We can identify perhaps ten people in the world who held Copernicus's view between 1543 and 1600.[1] It seems that Galileo was one of these ten.

≈

In 1597, Galileo's good friend from the University of Pisa, the philosopher Jacobo Mazzoni, had just written a book comparing Plato and Aristotle. He included in his book an all-too-easy argument against Copernicanism. Mazzoni sent the book to Galileo for comment. In Galileo's gentle chastisement of Mazzoni, we have his first clear espousal of Copernicanism.

But to tell the truth . . . I have been left . . . confused and intimidated upon seeing Your Most Worthy Excellency so resolute and frank in opposing the opinion of the Pythagoreans and of Copernicus concerning the motion and location of the Earth . . . and Your Excellency's reasoning has made me prick up my ears all the more since I have held the very opinion to be much more probable than that of Aristotle and Ptolemy and I have some feelings on this and other matters that flow from it.[2]

Galileo continued his letter by arguing for Copernicanism. He called Plato his (and Mazzoni's) master,[3] an indication that Galileo, too, had chosen Copernicanism because of its Neoplatonic associations.

But that isn't the only reason he thought Copernicanism likely. As early as 1595, Galileo had used the motion of the earth—its rotation on its own axis, and its yearly revolution around the sun—to explain the rising and ebbing of the tides, as had Copernicus.[4] The earth's motion produced a sort of sloshing of the seas in their basins.

Galileo was adamantly opposed to the explanation that the moon was somehow responsible for the tides. There is no plausible way, said Galileo, for the moon to affect the earth without coming into physical contact with it. To hypothesize a sort of mystical attraction from the moon would be to return to occult or hidden powers, like those prevalent in alchemy. Galileo later wrote in *The Assayer*:

The introduction of such lines is in no way superior to the "sympathy," "antipathy," "occult properties," "influences," and other terms employed by some philosophers for the correct reply, which would be: "I do not know." That reply is as much more tolerable than the others as candid honesty is more beautiful than deceitful duplicity.[5]

Newton would hear this same complaint from his own contemporaries when he spoke of gravitational attraction. In any case, Galileo's tidal explanation would become the linchpin of his argument for Copernicanism. Unfortunately, it was wrong.

Around the same time as his correspondence with Mazzoni, Galileo wrote a letter to the German astronomer Johannes Kepler, thanking him for a copy of his book *Mysterium Cosmographicum*. Kepler was another key figure in the scientific revolution. When Galileo wrote the letter, Kepler had no idea who Galileo was. Paul Hamberger, a friend of Kepler's, had carried with him to Italy two copies of the *Mysterium Cosmographicum* to place in the hands of people who mattered, and Hamberger chose Galileo.

Galileo immediately wrote Kepler:

I have already for many years come to accept the Copernican opinion, and with this hypothesis have been able to explain many natural phenomena, which under the current hypotheses remain unexplainable. I have written down many proofs and have undone the contrary arguments, but I have not yet dared to make these known because I have been frightened by the fate of our master Copernicus, who, although he gained an immortal fame among some, with an infinite number of others (how numerous are the stupid ones) he has been pushed aside and scorned. I would certainly not hesitate to put my thoughts out there, if there were more people around like you, but since there are not, I will forbear doing so.[6]

Kepler enthusiastically responded, encouraging Galileo to go public with his Copernican views. And, if he could, make some astronomical observations for him. Galileo did neither; he didn't even reply to Kepler's letter. Although they would eventually resume their correspondence, it wouldn't be for another thirteen years.

12

AN ILL WIND

Galileo was not only interested in science, but also in its application to engineering. Perhaps for financial reasons, he focused especially on military applications. Governments have always been willing to pay handsomely for military technology. Galileo cast about for ideas.

His first engineering opportunity had come in 1593, when the commander of the world-famous Venetian arsenal had asked him for advice on shipbuilding, in particular, on optimum oar arrangement.[1] An oar is essentially a lever, and Galileo's familiarity with Archimedian simple machines made him the ideal consultant.

Galileo also consulted on fortifications. And because many of Padua's students were preparing for military careers, Galileo began private tutoring on military architecture, including the best ways to assault and defend buildings. He also consulted on the trajectory of cannonballs; the shape of a cannonball's path would become important to Galileo's theoretical work in physics.

But the most lucrative of Galileo's military devices was his "geometric and military compass," developed around 1597.[2] Similar to the two-armed hinged device we use to draw circles, it was essentially a portable calculator, allowing engineers, soldiers, or sailors to solve any mathematical problem they were likely to encounter.[3] He made the compasses in his workshop located on the ground floor of the large house he now rented. The device was so successful that, in 1599, Galileo hired a craftsman to come live with him and make them full-time. Galileo also had the man bring his family with him.

By this time Galileo's home was a small inn, a boarding house for students and other guests. Boarders lived upstairs, while Galileo—and his workshop—occupied the first floor. His house became a lively gathering place, visitors participating in lectures, studying, manufacturing, and feasting. Perhaps not the ideal situation for silent contemplation, but Galileo enjoyed the debates and discussions. And though he needed the money, his generosity allowed him only to break even on the venture.

One person who may have come to live with Galileo was the young and beautiful Venetian Marina Gamba, whom he met in 1599.[4] Although they never married, their twelve-year love affair resulted in three children. The details about their relationship are sparse but provide enough to tempt speculation. Many scholars think that Galileo didn't marry Marina because he was a Florentine nobleman and she a lower-class foreigner. A marriage to Marina would have hurt his movement within the circles he frequented. It is interesting that an illicit lover would not have.

That same year—1599—university officials were considering the renewal of Galileo's teaching post. For help in the negotiations, Galileo turned to a well-connected Venetian patrician, Giovanfrancesco Sagredo. Sagredo, who would become Galileo's closest friend, was able to negotiate an increase from 180 florins to 320. Galileo's predecessor, Moletti, never got more than 300. One story—probably apocryphal—tells of how an enemy tried to use Galileo's relationship with Marina to block the contract's renewal. University officials replied that, on the contrary, Galileo would therefore need the job all the more—and *more* money.[5]

It is difficult, if not impossible, for us to reconcile a Christian behaving the way Galileo did toward Marina, no matter how devoted he was to her. We simply don't know all the details, and they might not change our judgment in any case. But biographer and Roman Catholic priest Michael Sharratt has written:

> Even inveterate opponents in later controversy did not suggest that by his irregular domestic arrangements Galileo had forfeited his claim to be counted as a good Catholic. They conceded that he was orthodox in intent, though misguided and too inclined to correspond with Protestants and other dubious characters. "Good Catholic" did not mean "exemplary Catholic": it just meant "definitely one of us," a fact which his many clerical friends, including cardinals, never had any reason to doubt.[6]

In any case, with respect to Marina, some biographers have excused Galileo on the one hand, or excoriated him on the other. But we can say this: regardless of cultural conventions, Galileo messed up. This is neither excusable nor entirely surprising. It was, however, tolerated.

～

Despite the tolerance that Venice worked to maintain—in academic, political, religious, and social matters—it had its limits. In 1592, just six months before Galileo arrived in Padua, the brilliant and eccentric Dominican, Giordono Bruno, was imprisoned in Venice by the Roman Inquisition on suspicion of heresy.[7] But even though Venice agreed to hand over Bruno to the Inquisition, it was only after the city was fully convinced that Bruno's views were heretical.[8] Bruno is now famous as a martyr for the cause of science, but he was actually condemned for beliefs about the nature of Christ, beliefs for which the Church had condemned others.[9] Nevertheless, Bruno was a Copernican, and this association no doubt brought heliocentricity under suspicion.

The Inquisition burned Bruno to death in 1600. From the sidelines in Padua, Galileo could hardly have failed to realize that ideas from the ivory tower could lead to real-life consequences.

The cultural climate of the sixteenth century was just right for Bruno's condemnation. Already by the middle of the 1500s, the Roman Catholic Church was taking measures against the charges and successes of the Protestant Reformers. The Church in Rome had become extrasensitive to matters of doctrine given the rapid spread of what they considered the Reformers' heresies. One of the ways to strengthen the influence of the Roman Church in Europe was through education and proselytizing, and as we saw, the Society of Jesus was founded primarily for this purpose.

But to address specific cases of heresy, in 1542 Pope Paul III established the Congregation of the Holy Office of the Inquisition, sometimes called simply the "Holy Office" or "Inquisition." There had been earlier inquisitions, the previous century's Spanish Inquisition (which was actually independent of Rome) being the most notorious. But the Roman Inquisition—the one that condemned Bruno—was established in response to "the great apostasy of the sixteenth century, the filtration of heresy into Catholic lands, and the progress of heterodox teachings everywhere."[10] It was a tribunal of six to thirteen cardinals and was "the final court of appeal for trials concerning faith."[11]

Perhaps the most significant measure taken by the Catholic Church began in 1545, again by Pope Paul III (to whom Copernicus had dedicated *De Revolutionibus* two years earlier in 1543).[12] The pope called a council, first held in the Italian Imperial city of Trent.[13] It was dismissed in 1563 after twenty-five sessions, and its decrees declared in 1564, the year Galileo was born.[14] The Council of Trent was Rome's definitive answer to the Reformation; it began the Counter-Reformation in earnest.

The printing press was one of the engines of the Protestant Reformation, and so books were closely watched. In 1571, the job of maintaining the *Index of Prohibited Books* was given to a special congregation, the Congregation of the Index. (Previously this was the Inquisition's responsibility.) All of Bruno's works were placed on the *Index* in 1603. It is telling that Copernicus's *De Revolutionibus* was not. It was still lawful to be a Copernican, even if not popular.

≈

Galileo's family responsibilities were increasing. His first daughter, Virginia, was born in 1600, when Galileo was thirty-six and Marina twenty-two. There had been a similar age difference between Galileo's father and mother. The parish in Padua registered Virginia as the "daughter of Marina from Venice" and as "born of fornication."[15] In 1601, Marina gave birth to Galileo's second daughter, Livia, and later, in 1606, to their third child, Vincenzio. (Galileo apparently had no sympathy for future biographers: he named his daughters after his sisters and his son after his father. Some biographers succumbed to putting Roman numerals after their names.)

In addition to providing for his immediate family, such as it was, Galileo had the added financial responsibility of his youngest sister's dowry. In 1601, Livia married Taddeo Galletti. Galileo had apparently negotiated a huge dowry to ensure that Livia would marry a respectable man. Again, he bought the wedding dress, and this time paid for the wedding feast.[16] The dowry, however, was a heavy long-term commitment. To put things in perspective, Galileo's yearly salary was 320 florins, or ducats. The dowry was 1,800 ducats, with 800 due at the time of the wedding and then 200 ducats to be paid yearly for the next five years.[17]

Galileo had expected his twenty-five-year-old brother, Michelangelo, to help with the installments. But at the time, Michelangelo was embarking on a career as a court musician, like his father. In 1600, he had moved to the court of a Polish prince. To pay his travel expenses, Michelangelo took a loan from Galileo.[18] When Galileo wrote to Michelangelo for help with the dowry, the only thing his little brother gave him was grief. Why, complained Michelangelo, had Galileo settled on such a large amount for their sister?

Galileo was remarkably patient with Michelangelo, and he was generous all around. At times he was generous with money he didn't have. In 1602, he had to get a two-year advance on his salary.[19]

Around this same time—probably in the summer of 1603—Galileo and two friends took an afternoon nap in a villa just outside Padua. They slept in a lower room cooled naturally by air from an underground cave. Viviani wrote:

> This wind, being excessively cold and damp, meeting with their very lightly clothed bodies during a time of two hours while they were reposing there, gradually introduced into them so bad a quality in their limbs that upon their awakening, one had torpor and chills, another intense headache and various disorders; all fell into grave illness of which one of them died in a few days, the second lost his hearing and did not survive a great time.[20]

Galileo, on the other hand, would suffer "up to the end of his life, by very severe pains and twinges that molested him bitterly at changes of weather, in various parts of this body."[21] Most likely, Galileo and his friends had breathed harmful gases, a common problem with such air conditioning and the reason these sorts of ancient ventilating ducts were sealed.[22]

It was an ill wind; from now on, he would struggle with his ailment, periodically bedridden for weeks.[23] But Galileo did not give in easily. Sometimes his writing was slanted, indicating that he tried to write even while lying down.[24] He was a fighter.

Although during his early years at Padua, Galileo spent most of his time on the invention of practical devices, he returned to his study of physics around 1602. He continued to refine some of the Aristotelian ideas he had laid out in *De Motu*, but he mostly traveled his own path.

Galileo discovered his famous "Law of Fall" at Padua. This new law is different from the Leaning Tower Law (his discovery that an object's rate of fall is independent of its weight). The Law of Fall is mathematical and says that the distance an object falls from rest is proportional to the square of the time that it falls. Not having algebraic notation, Galileo wrote it this way:

The spaces described by a body falling from rest with a uniformly accelerated motion are to each other as the squares of the time-intervals employed in traversing these distances.

This law is only true, strictly speaking, in a vacuum, or at least where air resistance is small enough to be ignored.

But objects fall very fast, so fast that it's difficult to even recognize variations in time, much less measure them. Even today this requires sophisticated devices, and in Galileo's time there was no way to measure small intervals of time.[25] One way that Galileo mitigated this problem was to use inclined planes for his "free fall" experiments. Rolling a smooth ball down an inclined plane slows the ball's speed, making it easier to measure its time. As Galileo made the incline steeper and steeper, he could extrapolate to the case of free fall (which is simply a "vertical" inclined plane).

Galileo also studied projectile motion. He discovered that any projectile's path is a parabola. Amazingly, this curved parabola is a simple combination of two independent straight-line motions—a constant-speed horizontal motion plus a naturally accelerating vertical motion. The horizontal motion is due to the "projector," an arm, a cannon, a bow. The vertical motion is simply due to the object's weight. The combination of two straight lines forming a curve is analogous to using an Etch A Sketch to draw a curved line with only horizontal and vertical motions, one knob controlling the horizontal motion, the other controlling the vertical motion.

The implications of this are surprising. Imagine firing a cannonball horizontally from a castle wall. Suppose that, at the same moment the cannon is fired horizontally, someone next to the cannon drops another cannonball from that same height. If the terrain is flat for miles around, the cannonball shot from the cannon will hit the ground at the same time as the cannonball that was dropped. The horizontal motion of the shot cannonball doesn't affect the vertical motion caused by its own weight.

The independence of these two motions is as helpful as it is amazing. The ability to break down a projectile's complicated motion into simpler, but imaginary, horizontal and vertical components makes the study of such motion much easier—we can have simpler mathematical descriptions for each component. Such unexpected simplifications suggest that the universe is user-friendly, almost as if it were made just for us.

But as intent as Galileo was on studying terrestrial laws of motion, celestial events began to distract him. In 1604, a new star appeared and, like the magi, Galileo followed it.

13

A STAR IS BORN

In 1572, when Galileo was a young boy, he was shown a bright, starlike object that had appeared in the Mediterranean sky. Like comets, the new object—this *nova*—caused a great stir in Europe. Such phenomena were still believed to be messengers or omens, sometimes with good news, but often bad.

The famous Danish astronomer Tycho Brahe (who wore a prosthetic metal nose to replace the original lost in a sword duel) made exacting measurements of the 1572 nova. Brahe, the most acclaimed astronomer of the last half of the 1500s, argued that the nova was outside the moon's sphere, in the celestial realm. This is no surprise to us, but to Aristotelians—which meant nearly everyone—the claim would have been astonishing. The celestial realm was eternal and unchanging, so new objects were forbidden. The very words *nova* (new) and *celestial* were contradictory. The Aristotelians, therefore, argued that the new object must be in the terrestrial realm, perhaps a collection of vapors in the upper atmosphere, just below the moon.

But Brahe had pointed out that if the nova were that close,

then—as with the moon—we should observe an apparent difference in its location against the backdrop of fixed stars, depending on where we are on the earth. An object's apparent difference in location relative to the constellations is called *parallax*, and this obscure and seemingly insignificant concept turns out to be a central concept in the history of astronomy, and therefore in the history of man. Unfortunately, Brahe was merely an astronomer, and so philosophers paid little attention.

In 1604, when another nova appeared, Brahe had been dead for three years. But this time the Aristotelians would pay attention to its implications. Galileo made sure of it.

Baldessar Capra and his German math tutor, Simon Mayr, were the first people in Padua to observe the nova. Galileo learned of it a couple of weeks later, on October 28, and was riveted.[1] For the first time, he began making his own observations and measurements of the heavens, while writing to others for additional measurements. Before this time, astronomy—observing, measuring, and calculating the positions of celestial objects—had never interested Galileo. He had taught astronomy only because he was obligated to as the mathematics professor.[2] He knew, however, that the nova had philosophical implications far outreaching its astronomical ones.

As always, the public was interested in the potential omen, giving Galileo the opportunity to present three open lectures on the nova.[3] Galileo's argument was essentially the same as Brahe's, but the argument found a much larger audience. Galileo had publicly thrown down the gauntlet.

His Aristotelian friend and Paduan colleague, Cesare

Cremonini, took it up. Cremonini immediately launched into his own public lectures against Galileo's position.[4] Cremonini also published *Discourse on the Nova*, under the pseudonym Antonio Lorenzini (a common practice at the time). Cremonini argued that the same kinds of measurements we make in the terrestrial realm—those relevant to parallax—aren't applicable to the celestial realm. The celestial realm behaves altogether differently.

Galileo responded in his own pseudonymous *Dialogue of Cecco di Ronchitti*, claiming that the measurements and calculations hold for any kind of material, even aether. In fact, Galileo continued, the new star could be made out of cornmeal, for all mathematicians care.

In 1605, Galileo had another public exchange with an Aristotelian, this time Ludovico delle Colombe. Colombe argued that the star had always been there but was normally so small and dim that it couldn't be seen. The star was then magnified when a small lenslike portion in a crystalline sphere moved in between us and the star as the sphere rotated.[5] This was exactly the type of ad hoc Aristotelian ploy that Galileo hated.[6] He responded in 1606 with his *Considerations of Alimberto Mauri on some Passages in the Discourse of Lodivico* [sic] *delle Colombe*. After a year of searching, Colombe couldn't find anyone by the name of Alimberto Mauri and correctly inferred that the author was Galileo Galilei, his new enemy.

≈

During most of the university's breaks, Galileo would return to Florence. As much as he enjoyed Padua and Venice, he was a Florentine at heart, and he wished his body and heart to be together. In 1605, Galileo accepted an invitation from the Grand Duchess Christina to tutor her son, Cosimo II. Among the topics on which Galileo instructed Cosimo was the geometric and military compass. Galileo told Cosimo of his plans to formally publish an instruction manual on the device, and promised to dedicate it to the young prince.

The reason for publishing a manual was to protect his intellectual property, not to make money from its sales. Typically, Galileo personally instructed students on the compass, giving them manuals handwritten by a hired amanuensis or secretary. But as the students—many of them foreign—returned to their homes, news of his invention spread, along with instructions of its use.[7] In order, therefore, to establish his priority with the invention, he hired a printer and produced sixty copies of the manual out of his home.

Galileo's concern about intellectual theft was prophetic. The man who had first viewed the nova in Padua, Baldessar Capra, plagiarized Galileo's booklet in 1607, rewriting and rearranging the material in Latin. Most of the book was probably written by his tutor, Simon Mayr, for it turned out that Capra didn't understand all of the technical details contained in the manual. Galileo discovered this while cross-examining Capra in court.[8] Galileo was vindicated by the university governors, and Capra was expelled from the university.[9]

During the summer of 1608, the Grand Duchess Christina insisted that Galileo attend eighteen-year-old Cosimo's wedding to Maria Magdalena, the archduchess of Austria. Within months, Cosimo's father, the Grand Duke Ferdinando fell ill, and Christina asked Galileo to cast a horoscope for him. It wasn't uncommon for Christians to have horoscopes cast, since astrology was still part of astronomy. Galileo—who had cast horoscopes before—had good news: the duke would recover from his illness. Ferdinando died a few weeks later in February 1609, and Cosimo assumed the throne.

Regardless of the bad news of Ferdinando's death, Galileo's former pupil was in a position of power. This, at least, was a good thing, for Galileo wanted the position of Tuscan court mathematician. He was tired of teaching (especially private tutoring, which he called "prostitution"[10]) and wished to devote his studies to research and publishing.

In between bouts of illness and other distractions, Galileo would work on his new science of motion. But the nova of 1604 had already watered down his efforts. Soon, the direction of his scientific work would change entirely, and he would not return to physics for many years.[11]

14

DESEGREGATION

1609 was momentous for the smoldering scientific revolution. That year Kepler published his *Astronomia Nova*, bringing an end to millennia of fussing with the planets' meandering paths. Since Plato, philosophers and astronomers alike had assumed that they could analyze the paths of the heavenly bodies in terms of circles and constant speed. They had paid dearly for this assumption in time and toil. And though Copernicus's system reduced the number of circles upon circles, it was still "monstrous." Ironically, Copernicus couldn't simplify things further because he was intent on keeping the simplicity of circular motion at a constant speed.

In the *Astronomia Nova*, Kepler reduced the muddle of circles to a single elliptical path for each planet, with the sun located at one of the foci, one of the two "centers" of the ellipse. In addition, Kepler reported that a planet moves faster as it gets nearer the sun, slowing down as it moves away.

Galileo rejected Kepler's elliptical motion. Planetary orbits are very nearly circular (they certainly look circular when plotted on paper), but when it came to mathematical astronomy and the prediction of exact locations of planets, every little bit mattered. But Galileo—whose interest in the heavens was more philosophical than mathematical—could tolerate small deviations.[1]

There may have also been another reason Galileo rejected Kepler's claims. Galileo was uncomfortable with the way Kepler "philosophized." Galileo believed that Kepler was a bit too cavalier, even mystical, especially with respect to his Pythagorean commitments. This is ironic, because it was Galileo's own Pythagoreanism—his own faith in the mathematical structure of nature—that made him choose perfect circular orbits over elliptical ones. Not even a man like Galileo could take everything in. Too much was changing too quickly.

But 1609's second momentous event had little to do with Kepler or mathematical astronomy. Rather, it had important cosmological ramifications, implications about the very composition and structure of the cosmos, and it led to an observational discovery that unified the *uni*verse.

≈

The year before, a spectacle maker, Hans Lipperhey, had applied to the Dutch government for a patent on a device that could make distant objects appear much closer than they actually were—a "spyglass." The Netherlands denied the patent because it was too easy to copy. News of the device spread quickly, and by July 1609 Galileo had heard of it from his friar friend Paolo Sarpi, while visiting Venice.[2]

Galileo was still struggling financially, continually campaigning for better pay or a better position. He immediately realized the military value of a spyglass, especially for a maritime power such as Venice. Galileo rushed back to his workshop in Padua "to inquire into the means by which I might arrive at the invention of a similar instrument."[3]

Galileo then heard of a stranger visiting Venice, attempting to sell a spyglass to the Venetian Senate. The foreigner was asking for one thousand ducats; he also asked that the spyglass never be taken apart for inspection. Galileo's friend Sarpi advised the government against buying the device, perhaps telling them that Galileo could make a better one.

And Galileo could. Near the end of August, Galileo took his own eight-powered instrument to Venice for demonstration. In a letter to his brother-in-law (the same one who had threatened Galileo with imprisonment), Galileo relayed how he had showed the spyglass to

> the entire Senate, to the infinite amazement of all; and there have been numerous gentlemen and senators who, though old, have more than once climbed the stairs of the highest campaniles in Venice to observe at sea sails and vessels so far away that, coming under fully sail to port, two hours and more were required before they could be seen without my spyglass. For in fact the effect of this instrument is to represent an object that is for example fifty miles away as large and near as if it were but five.[4]

He went on to say,

> I resolved on the 25th of this month to appear in the College
> and make a free gift of it to his Lordship [the Doge of Venice].
> And having been ordered to wait in the room of the Pregadi,
> there appeared presently the Procurator Priuli, who is one of
> the governors of the University. Coming out of the College,
> he took my hand and told me how that body . . . would at
> once order the honorable governors that, if I were content,
> they should renew my appointment for life and with a salary
> of one thousand florins per year . . . to run immediately . . .
> Thus I find myself here, held for life, and shall have to be
> satisfied to enjoy my native land sometimes during the sum-
> mer months.[5]

But when Galileo received the actual renewal contract for
his Paduan post, the fine print indicated that he would have
to wait until the end of his current contract, which still had a
year remaining. Moreover, the contract prohibited any future
increase in salary.

Galileo's financial responsibilities must have been particularly pressing, for despite the guarantee of a handsome financial
package—almost twice his current salary—he renewed his cam-
paign for the court mathematician in Florence. (Ricci had died
in 1603, leaving the post vacant.)[6] As long as he hadn't received
any actual benefits from the new contract, Galileo felt within his
rights to seek new employment. But this was a dangerous game.

The Venetian government had just shown their commitment to Galileo, and—with respect to the Tuscan court—Galileo had just given a foreign nation powerful military technology. If Galileo didn't play this carefully, all could be lost.

He paid a quick visit—probably in October 1609, before the school year began—to the Grand Duke Cosimo, showing him the instrument and perhaps smoothing over any ill will.[7] Cosimo was impressed and told Galileo that he wouldn't mind having a spyglass of his very own. While in Florence, Galileo quickly procured high-quality glass blanks and returned to Padua. It was during this time that we get a small glimpse of his mother's personality. She wrote to Galileo's servant, asking him to steal a few lenses; Galileo wouldn't miss them. And by the way, was there any household gossip that he might send along with the lenses?[8]

≈

Galileo eventually made a twenty-power spyglass—the word *telescope* had still not been coined—and made perhaps the most obvious yet unexpected move: he pointed the spyglass at the heavens. He made a rapid series of astonishing observations in December and January. In March 1610, he published his telescopic discoveries in the *Sidereal Nuncius*, or *Starry Messenger*, a pamphlet dedicated "To the Most Serene Cosimo II de´ Medici Fourth Grand Duke of Tuscany."[9]

The starry message was very bad news for Aristotelians, with implications similar to that of the nova of 1604. In his pamphlet Galileo reported what he had already guessed: the moon was not a perfect sphere. He saw—the first human ever to do so—mountains and craters covering the moon. The darker spots had always been interpreted as optical illusions created by the earth's atmosphere.[10] Galileo also discovered that the Milky Way was composed of innumerable fixed stars, but this wasn't nearly as significant as a mountainous and pockmarked moon. The moon, according to the philosophers, was perfectly smooth, made out of immaculate aether. But Galileo claimed that the moon was made of material similar to—perhaps identical with—the four terrestrial elements. Galileo even compared the moon's mountains to those in Bohemia.

Furthermore, Galileo claimed, the moon shone because it reflected the light of the sun and earth, not because it was made from a luminescent fifth element. It seemed, then, that the terrestrial and celestial realms were one and the same. This was a difficult inference to avoid, and so Galileo didn't. Galileo's starry message was a proclamation for the world to unite; it was one of desegregation.

This amounted to philosophical heresy for Aristotelians.[11] As Drake has commented:

> Even in antiquity the idea that the moon (or any other heavenly body) was of the same nature as the earth had been dangerous to hold. The Athenians banished the philosopher Anaxagoras for teaching such notions, and charged Socrates with blasphemy for repeating them.[12]

As Galileo would learn, crossing philosophers can be just as dangerous as crossing theologians.

The desegregation of the cosmos would have one of the most profound impacts on the study of nature. If the heavens were like the earth, then no longer would we need a set of laws for terrestrial physics and another for the heavens; a single set of physical laws would suffice. Furthermore, experiments performed on earth could tell us about the behavior of the stars. The motion of a cannonball could tell us about the motion of Venus.[13]

But the *Starry Messenger* bore more bad news for Aristotelians: Jupiter had its own satellites. Galileo reported that four little stars orbited the much larger Jovian wanderer. These additional wandering stars—which Galileo strategically named the *Medicean Stars*—immediately destroyed the earth's uniqueness. Other objects could own satellites too. It was this discovery that disturbed the Aristotelians most. If Jupiter moved, yet had satellites, the fact that the earth had its own moon did not imply that the earth was stationary.[14] Satellites could have satellites.

Galileo was aware of his discoveries' significance. Similar to the discoveries of the Americas a century earlier, Galileo had exposed and explored a new world. The English scientist Sir William Lower wrote:

> Me thinks my diligent Galileus hath done more in his three fold discourie than Magellane in opening the streightes to the Sout sea or the dutch men that weare eaten by beares in noua Zembla.[15]

The Scottish poet Thomas Seggett expressed Lower's thoughts more eloquently and with better spelling:

Columbus gave man lands to conquer by bloodshed,
Galileo new worlds harmful to none.
Which is better?[16]

Galileo wished to further explore the implications of his discoveries, but there was something missing: time.[17] His teaching obligations consumed most of his nonwaking hours. And then there were his frequent bouts of illness. Galileo needed to be Tuscany's court mathematician.

Galileo sent Cosimo a copy of the *Starry Messenger* as well as the telescope he had used for the observations described in it.[18] Of course, Galileo would have to visit the grand duke to assist him in using it. In April, during Easter break, Galileo traveled to Pisa, where the court spent the winter, showing Cosimo the stars named in his honor.[19]

〜

Although Galileo's spyglass provided a new way to investigate philosophical claims, novelty wasn't a virtue particularly valued by philosophers. The ancients had pointed the way, and philosophy, the Aristotelians believed, was primarily a matter of studying the texts of the master. In fact, there were philosophers who simply refused to take the time to look through the spyglass. Galileo's philosopher friend at Padua, Cremonini, was one of these, as was the main Pisan philosopher, Giulio Libri. When Libri died in 1610, Galileo remarked that since Libri hadn't seen the discoveries while he was on earth, perhaps he would get a chance on the way to heaven.[20]

In all fairness to the philosophers, they didn't have the benefit of centuries of observational astronomy under their belts. Nor was there a fully developed theory of optics. This resulted in some skepticism of the spyglass's reliability. In fact, the ancient historian Plutarch had expressed doubts about lenses in general.[21] The influential Jesuit mathematician in Rome, Christopher Clavius, initially believed that the phenomena observed were in the lenses. This perhaps explains, in part, why neither Cremonini nor Libri would look through them (although Cremonini claimed it would give him a headache). And the cost of trusting these mysterious little lenses was very high. An entire worldview would have to be given up on the basis of a few observations reported by a single mathematician. It would be best to wait before accepting such dramatic claims. Time would tell.

Some philosophers made desperate ad hoc defenses of Aristotelian cosmology. For example, Ludovico delle Colombe (and others) acknowledged the moon's mountains and craters but still defended its perfect smoothness. The moon, they said, was covered in a smooth, invisible coat of aether.[22] This, of course, would be impossible for Galileo to directly refute. So he didn't try. He simply said, "The hypothesis is pretty; its only fault is that [it] is neither demonstrated nor demonstrable."[23]

But Galileo received unequivocal support from the well-respected Kepler in *Conversation with Galileo's Sidereal Messenger*.[24] This was important, especially now. The Tuscan ambassador to Venice had reported back to the grand duke that Galileo was being laughed at and that he had tricked the Venetian government into giving him an inordinate sum for a device that could be easily copied.[25]

≈

In May 1610, Galileo wrote to Cosimo's secretary of state, Belisario Vinta, to follow up on the position of court mathematician. He assured Vinta that the grand duke need no longer worry about the doubts of his telescopic discoveries. Galileo had just given three lectures in Padua and convinced the whole university of his discoveries. Galileo also noted that he had a very long letter of approval from Kepler, the astronomer to the Holy Roman Empire.

Galileo went on to discuss his terms of employment: a salary of 1,000 florins (far more than Vinta himself made; Ostillio Ricci had made only 144)[26] and sufficient time for research and writing. He also asked that he be legally absolved of his brother Michelangelo's portion of their sister's dowries. And, "Finally," Galileo requested, "as to the title and scope of my duties, I wish in addition to the name of Mathematician that his Highness adjoin that of Philosopher."[27]

The duke granted all of his requests, and in October 1610, Galileo would officially begin his lifelong appointment as "Chief Mathematician at the University of Pisa and Philosopher and Mathematician to the Grand Duke."[28] This time there was no troublesome fine print. And the position at the University of Pisa entailed no teaching whatsoever. It was a position that provided prestige in return for no effort at all. This was a dream job that would provoke university philosophers to jealousy. And this jealousy would have consequences. The philosophers' envy alone was enough to provide the motive for attacks on Galileo. Add to that Galileo's eventual demolition of their philosophy, and Galileo became a living target.

That summer, while Galileo was preparing to move back to Florence, he continued his telescopic observations. He discovered that Saturn has an oblong shape. Or perhaps these were two satellites; it was difficult to tell. Saturn is much farther away than Jupiter, and Galileo's telescope was too weak to see any more than an oblong blur. Galileo sent Kepler an anagram or coded statement of his observations of Saturn. By sending the anagram without the solution, Galileo could establish his priority without going public before he was ready. If his priority was challenged, he could call upon Kepler to back up his claim. This was a common strategy, and Newton, too, would send codes to safeguard his reputation. There is, after all, a reason for intellectual property laws.

15

THE PAX ROMANA

We have little information about Galileo's family during this time. A year earlier, in 1609, he had sent his oldest daughter, Virginia, to live with his mother, Giulia, in Florence. This may have been at the old woman's insistence. Giulia had visited Galileo while he was playing with his telescopes and felt sorely neglected.[1] Galileo, she may have thought, was too distracted to be a good father. And his frequent illnesses only made matters worse. Whatever the circumstances, for Galileo to allow Virginia to live with her grandmother, things must have been bad indeed.

When Galileo moved from Padua back to Florence in September 1610, he brought Virginia's nine-year-old sister, Livia, with him.[2] Four-year-old Vincenzio stayed with his mother, Marina, who would marry Giovanni Bartoluzzi soon after Galileo moved away. It was Galileo, in fact, who arranged the marriage, even helping Bartoluzzi find a job. Galileo would eventually send for Vincenzio too; but for now, he sent child support.[3]

Galileo's recurring disability was probably the source for many of his familial decisions. And his health would only get worse upon his return to Florence.

> After the absence of so many years, I have experienced the very thin air of Florence as a cruel enemy of my head and the rest of my body. Colds, discharges of blood, and constipation have during the last three months reduced me to such a state of weakness, depression, and despondency that I have been practically confined to the house, or rather to my bed, but without the blessing of sleep or rest.[4]

Although Galileo would occasionally find relief by staying at his friend Filippo Salviati's villa outside of Florence, his illness was chronic and his family would suffer from his sickness almost as much as he did.[5] Later, his daughter Virginia's letters would be filled with concern for her father's health.

There were other family problems. Michelangelo would make occasional appearances in his older brother's life, but only as a burden or bother. When Galileo sent a copy of the *Starry Messenger* to the Elector of Cologne, the elector requested a telescope. From Germany, Michelangelo threw the following tantrum:

> See if you can gratify the Elector by showing him how to manufacture the instrument; and if not, write him a letter in your own way . . . You say not a word about the telescope I asked you for. And if I am not a prince able to remunerate

you, at any rate I am your brother, and it seems very strange to me that you do not care to gratify me with this thing. Pray send me the cords [lute strings] without fail; and above all, do not forget, when you go to Florence, to procure me letters of recommendation from the Grand Duke to my master; but mind you, let them be good ones, such as you know how to get easily enough. I have nothing more to say, except that I beg you not to forget what I have asked for.[6]

What, after all, are big brothers for?

~

In December, Galileo received good news from the Jesuit front. Clavius—now seventy—had finally seen Jupiter's satellites. Apparently, the Jesuits at the Collegio Romano had a new and stronger telescope. Clavius sent Galileo congratulations: "Truly Your Lordship deserves much praise since you are the first to have observed this."[7] In Galileo's reply to Clavius, he revealed yet another discovery, one that, this time, told directly against the Aristotelian view that all the planets rotate about the earth (and not simply against the terrestrial/celestial distinction):

And now you can see, my Lord, how we have ascertained that Venus (and indubitably Mercury will do the same) goes about the Sun, the center without any doubt of the principal revolutions of all planets. Furthermore we are certain of how those planets are of themselves dark and they shine only by illumination from the Sun (which I do not believe happens, from some of my observations, in the case of the fixed stars).[8]

Earlier that month Galileo had sent another anagram to Kepler in Prague with his observation that Venus goes through phases just as the earth's moon does. The anagram was "The mother of love emulates the figures of Cynthia [the moon]."[9] (Kepler tried desperately—and unsuccessfully—to decipher the message.[10]) Phases would be impossible unless Venus orbited the sun. And this raised the possibility that other planets did the same.

And to Galileo, this was more than a mere possibility; it was now a fact. Venus had cinched it.[11] On New Year's Day 1611, Galileo wrote the Tuscan ambassador to Prague, confidently explaining how Venus's phases show that it orbits "around the sun, as do also Mercury and all the other planets—something indeed believed by the Pythagoreans, Copernicus, Kepler, and myself."[12]

But even the revolution of Venus and the other wandering stars around the sun didn't point *definitively* to a moving earth. There was a third cosmological view—in addition to the Aristotelian and Copernican views—that would become popular. This *tertium quid* was Tycho Brahe's system of compromise, the "Tychonic" system.

Brahe had argued against Aristotelianism with his observations of novae and comets; he also believed that the planets revolved around the sun. Yet he still refused to accept a moving earth. In Brahe's system the sun orbited the earth while the planets orbited the sun. The entire swirling solar system was a satellite of the earth.

Galileo was well aware of Brahe's compromise but thought it was physically impossible, even though the Tychonic system was *mathematically* equivalent to Copernicus's.[13] Galileo reasoned that whatever caused all those planets to move around the sun would be too strong to leave the earth motionless.[14] But Galileo's reasoning, as it stood, seemed little more than prejudice. Or perhaps it was a genius's physical intuition. The two are often so difficult to distinguish.

~

In March 1611, despite his poor health, Galileo traveled to the Eternal City "in order to put an end, once and for all, to malignant rumors" regarding his discoveries.[15] Even with the six-day journey, he arrived in decent health.[16] The next day Galileo met with Clavius and the other Jesuit mathematicians. Clavius knew that the Aristotelian system was no longer entirely tenable but was still not convinced of Copernicanism. And Galileo did not press the point. In a show of tact and graciousness, he contented himself with Clavius's support of his observations, if not his interpretation of them. Regarding his conversation with Clavius, Galileo wrote that

> it would have been little less than a sacrilege to tire and trouble with discourses and comments an old man so venerable for his age, doctrine and goodness; he has with so many and such illustrious efforts gained an immortal reputation.[17]

Galileo was fond of the old man, and his comments here suggest that winning an argument wasn't always his main priority. Yet today, many of Galileo's critics castigate him as a Copernican zealot who would stop at nothing to spread the Copernican gospel.[18]

In any case, the Jesuits fully acknowledged Galileo's discoveries and considered him an esteemed scientist. The Jesuits honored Galileo with an elaborate academic conference at the Collegio Romano. The keynote address was "The Sidereal Message of the Roman College," in which a Belgian Jesuit, Odo Van Maelcote, approvingly presented Galileo's remarkable observations.[19]

It seems that Galileo also discussed his telescopic discoveries with the man at the helm of the Collegio Romano. Sixty-eight-year-old Jesuit cardinal Robert Bellarmine was the official theologian to the pope. Bellarmine—an amateur astronomer[20]—wrote to Clavius and the Jesuit mathematicians regarding the legitimacy of Galileo's astonishing discoveries:

> I am aware that Your Reverences have news of the new celestial observations of a worthy mathematician by means of an instrument called a cannon or an ocular; and moreover I have seen, by means of the same instrument, some very marvelous things about the Moon and Venus. But I wish you to do me the favor of telling me sincerely your opinion . . . I want to know this because I hear various opinions

being spoken about this matter; and since Your reverences
are occupied with the mathematical sciences, you will easily
be able to tell me whether these new inventions are well-
founded or whether they are apparent and not true.[21]

The mathematicians assured Bellarmine that Galileo's observations were genuine, although they pointed out that Clavius still
had doubts about the interpretation of the moon's craters and
mountains.

Cardinal Bellarmine's letter shows no signs of hostility or
suspicion toward Galileo, but his eventual role in Galileo's trial
makes his first mention of Galileo's discoveries noteworthy.
Bellarmine was the theological watchdog for the Church in
Rome and the leading theologian of the Counter-Reformation.
Other than the pope, he was probably the most hated Catholic
among the Protestants, especially in England.[22] To the English
he was a "byword and a bugaboo," "a petulant raile," "the head
of the popish kennel of Monks and Mendicants," and "a furious
and devilish Jebusite."[23] One verse chided:

First to breakfast, then to dine,
Is to conquer Bellarmine.[24]

Whatever this meant, it wasn't good.

The Protestants feared Bellarmine because of his fiery zeal
and considerable talents as a Catholic apologist. He was, after
all, a Jesuit, a soldier of the Church, and a hardened one at that.
He had fought with the Venetian Senate, Neapolitan Primatists,

Callicans, Lutherans, Anglicans, and Calvinists.[25] Bellarmine had also been one of the cardinals of the Inquisition when it condemned Bruno, and he was naturally concerned with heresies. He had written three volumes on the topic, in which he said:

> Let me say this one thing; the perversity of heretics is as much worse than all other evils and afflictions as the dreadful and fearful plague is worse than the more common diseases.[26]

Bellarmine was not to be trifled with, but neither was he unreasonable or rash. And in any case, Bellarmine's interest in Galileo's discoveries was philosophical and avocational rather than theological.

≈

While in Rome, Galileo was also honored by the *Accademia dei Lincei*, or Academy of the Lynx-eyed (those who can see clearly in the darkness). Academies—like the Florentine Academy—were popular outlets for literary and artistic discussions. But the Lyncean Academy was unique. In 1603, its founder, Prince Federico Cesi, established the group to discuss mostly scientific and mathematical issues.[27] It was the world's first scientific society, predating even England's Royal Society, which is usually considered the first genuinely scientific organization. The Lynceans feted Galileo at a banquet during his stay, honoring him with admission to the academy. In fact, it was during the banquet that someone—perhaps Cesi himself—suggested that Galileo's spyglass be called a *telescope*.[28]

Before Galileo left Rome, the Tuscan ambassador arranged for him to have an audience with Pope Paul V. The pope treated Galileo with uncommon respect, and Galileo wrote to his friend Salviati of this honor:

> This morning I went to pay my *respects* to his Holiness, and I was introduced by His Excellency our illustrious Ambassador, who told me that I had been treated with exceptional favor because his Holiness would not let me say a word kneeling but immediately commanded me to stand up.[29]

Galileo went on to tell Salviati of the overall success of his three-month Roman vacation: "I have been received and feted by many illustrious cardinals, prelates and princes who wanted to see the things I have observed and were much pleased."[30]

The trip could not have gone much better. Cardinal Francesco Maria del Monte, brother of Galileo's friend Guidobaldo, wrote to Cosimo:

> Galileo has, during his stay in Rome, given great satisfaction, and I think he received as much . . . Were we still living under the ancient republic of Rome, I am certain that a statue would have been erected in his honor on the Capitol.[31]

In June 1611, Galileo returned to Florence a hero. Indeed, this was his *pax Romana*, his own peace in Rome. But like the first *pax Romana*, it could not last.

16

A NEW FRIEND

In October 1611, Cosimo gave a dinner in honor of two visiting cardinals, Ferdinando Gonzaga and Maffeo Barberini. Cosimo also invited Galileo to debate a philosophy professor from the University of Pisa on the issue of floating bodies. Galileo's skill of oral debate had become renowned. One contemporary described Galileo's devastating method:

> Before answering the adversaries' arguments he amplified and reinforced them with apparently very powerful evidence which then made his adversaries look more ridiculous when he eventually destroyed their positions.[1]

Galileo thoroughly trounced the visiting philosophy professor, who no doubt appreciated having his errors corrected in front of a crowd. The goal was truth, after all.

Cardinal Barberini—a fellow Florentine—took Galileo's side. Barberini was a student of natural philosophy and had been put in charge of the Vatican's water supply.[2] He soon became an ardent admirer of Galileo's work. Just after the dinner debate, Galileo was again bedridden, and a week or so after his visit, Barberini wrote with concern:[3]

> I am very sorry that you were unable to see me before I left the city. It is not that I consider a sign of your friendship necessary, for it is well known to me, but because you were ill. May God keep you not only because outstanding persons, such as yourself, deserve a long life of public service, but because of the particular affection that I have and always will have for you. I am happy to be able to say this, and to thank you for the time that you spent with me.
>
> > Your affectionate brother,
> > Cardinal Barberini[4]

This letter, and its sentiments, would become important in the drama soon to unfold around Galileo. Cardinal Barberini would become Pope Urban VIII.

Biographer Dava Sobel points out that Barberini was in Florence to visit two nieces at a local convent. This may have been part of the reason that Galileo began to plan for his own daughters—now ten and eleven—to become nuns. Normally, sisters were prohibited to remain together in the same convent, but here was a case in which that rule had been broken. And Galileo absolutely did not want the sisters to be separated.

Joining a convent, then, seemed to Galileo the best course for his daughters' futures. They were illegitimate and therefore would have no real marriage prospects. Galileo's frequent bouts with illness—especially the most recent one—probably added support to the argument. Also, Galileo's mother was getting too old to bear the responsibility of helping him raise the girls. And she was insufferable. Galileo's sisters, Virginia and Livia, simply had too many of their own family responsibilities for him to impose two more children on them.[5]

Although the official age of taking religious vows was sixteen, the girls could still enter the convent early to prepare for their initiation. This was a common practice, and Sobel says that "fully 50 per cent of the daughters of Florentine patrician families spent at least part of their lives within convent walls."[6] In fact, Galileo's own sisters had done something similar, though they had both left to marry before taking vows. And so Galileo began looking into the matter.

~

Although the debate over floating bodies had gained Galileo an important friend in Cardinal Barberini, it also resulted in more enemies. In 1612, when Galileo finally published his views in *Discourse on objects which rest on water or which move in it*, it provoked a number of written attacks from Pisan and Florentine Aristotelians. Because Ludovico delle Colombe was the most prominent of these, this group was named after him: the *pigeon league*. Colombe's name meant "dove" or "pigeon" and this suited the Galieists just fine; *pigeon* also meant "simpleton" or "bird-brained."[7]

That year Galileo brought his son Vincenzio—now seven

years old—to Florence from Padua.[8] Meanwhile the philosophical attacks continued. One of the new philosophical disputes involved the sun itself. The Chinese had known about sunspots for centuries, but Europe had only just discovered them.[9] In 1612—in a series of letters—Galileo argued about the nature of these spots with a Jesuit astronomer from Germany, Christopher Scheiner. Scheiner, who began the exchange, believed that the spots were planets. Galileo, on the other hand, argued that they were on the surface of the sun. He also reported that the spots changed with time and that the sun rotated about once a month.

As troublesome as the sun's corruptibility might have been to an Aristotelian like Scheiner, he was more concerned that he receive credit for discovering the sunspots. In 1613, when the Lyncean Academy published Galileo's *Letters on the Sunspots*— with the *Imprimatur* or permission of the Church—the Lyncean secretary included a contentious preface insisting on Galileo's priority of the discovery. Galileo, shown the draft of the preface by Prince Cesi, worried that it would only aggravate matters. But Cesi convinced Galileo to ignore his instincts.

Galileo's instincts were correct; the Jesuits howled in protest.[10] Until now Galileo had been very careful to avoid unnecessary conflict with the Jesuits. Priority disputes often turned ugly because they amounted to accusations of intellectual theft. Ironically, in July 1613, Kepler pointed out that neither Scheiner nor Galileo were the first to observe sunspots. That honor went to Johann Fabricius.[11] That didn't, however, settle the matter. The charges had already been leveled, and some wounds heal more slowly than others.

THE THEOLOGICAL TURN

While attempting to get the Church's *Imprimatur* for the *Letters on the Sunspots*, Galileo learned that Catholic authorities were touchy when it came to any use of Scripture in published works. Before the censors finally gave Galileo permission to publish the *Letters on the Sunspots*, they made him revise it several times. It was his first face-to-face meeting with the workings of the Counter-Reformation.[1] Yet despite the censors' prickliness toward the explicit use of Scripture, they let Galileo's espousal of Copernicanism pass without comment.[2]

More theological clouds gathered when, in November 1612, Galileo heard that an elderly Dominican, Father Niccolò Lorini, had attacked the motion of the earth as being contrary to the Bible. Lorini assured Galileo, however, that he had only chimed in on the conversation "to show I was alive," although he admitted to saying that "the opinion of Ipernicus, or whatever his name is appears to be against Holy Scripture."[3]

Galileo wrote to Prince Cesi regarding Lorini's ignorance:

THE THEOLOGICAL TURN | 111

"But this good fellow is so unfamiliar with the founder of that doctrine that he calls him 'Ipernicus.' Now your Excellency can see how and from whom poor philosophy is jolted."[4] Galileo's criticism wasn't new. Copernicus, too, had complained that some theologians made rash pronouncements on Scripture's claims about nature. In the fourth century, Copernicus pointed out, Lactantius had proclaimed that the earth was flat.[5] But the Church had never made such views on natural philosophy official Christian doctrine.[6] And at this point, it still hadn't.

In December 1613, Galileo received a letter from his close friend Benedetto Castelli. Castelli, a Benedictine monk, now held Galileo's former chair of mathematics at Pisa. Castelli had studied with Galileo in Padua and collaborated with him on scientific work.[7] Castelli had also lived at Galileo's boarding house, where he was treated as one of the family.

Galileo had recommended Castelli for the chair at Pisa. It is astounding that Castelli was approved, given the hostility that the university's philosophy professors bore toward Galileo. Thankfully, mathematics wasn't philosophy. But Castelli was sternly warned by the university not to teach Copernicanism, to which Castelli replied that Galileo had already warned him of the same thing. Perhaps in defense of Galileo, Castelli also quipped that Galileo had never—in more than twenty years of teaching—taught his students that the earth moved.[8]

Castelli wrote to Galileo as he would "a father," relaying the events of a recent breakfast with the grand duke and his family. The Tuscan court was in Pisa for their yearly winter sojourn and had invited Castelli to their residence. Also in attendance at the breakfast were the grand duke's wife, his mother, and the philosopher Cosimo Boscaglia, whom the Medicis admired and protected.[9]

During the meal, conversation turned to the Medicean stars, Jupiter's satellites. Boscaglia acknowledged that these were real and not illusions produced by the telescope's lenses.[10] In fact, all of Galileo's observations were genuine, Boscaglia said; it was simply that Galileo's interpretations of them were wrong. In particular, "the motion of the Earth seemed incredible and could not be true, all the more so since Holy Scripture was clearly against this opinion."[11]

After the meal the discussion was resumed, and Cosimo's mother, the Dowager Grand Duchess Christina, sided with Boscaglia. She asked Father Castelli to speak on the matter as a theologian and not as a mathematician. In particular, she asked about the following passage in Joshua, chapter 10:

> Then Joshua spoke to the LORD in the day when the LORD delivered up the Amorites before the sons of Israel, and he said in the sight of Israel,
>
> "O sun, stand still at Gibeon,
> And O moon in the valley of Aijalon."
> So the sun stood still, and the moon stopped,
> Until the nation avenged themselves of their enemies.
>
> Is it not written in the book of Jashar? And the sun stopped in the middle of the sky and did not hasten to go *down* for about a whole day.[12]

Castelli responded that whenever there is a question about the exact workings of nature, we should defer to those who know nature best—natural philosophers—and not theologians. Then, *given these findings*, theologians should determine the meaning of such biblical passages.[13]

Although Father Castelli was confident that he had dealt decisively with the issue, Galileo was not so sure. In any case, the incident was serious enough for Galileo to formulate his own response—his views had been attacked in front of his employers.

Galileo quickly wrote a letter to Castelli on the relation between natural philosophy and Scripture. Galileo's fundamental assumption was that "the Holy Scripture can never lie or err, and that its declarations are absolutely and inviolably true."[14] Nevertheless, he continued,

> though Scripture cannot err . . . some of its interpreters and expositors can sometimes err in various ways. One of these would be very serious and very frequent, namely, to want to limit oneself always to the literal meaning of the words; for there would thus emerge not only various contradictions but also serious heresies and blasphemies, and it would be necessary to attribute to God feet, hands, and eyes, as well as bodily and human feelings like anger, regret, hate, and sometimes even forgetfulness of things past and ignorance of future ones.[15]

It is clear, said Galileo, that Scripture doesn't always speak literally. And depending on the topic, it could be a grave mistake to take a figurative passage for a literal one.

But there is another kind of case, Galileo wrote, where the correct interpretation of Scripture is the literal one, and yet Scripture is still not describing the actual underlying structure of nature. In such cases, the Holy Spirit is—as in the Joshua passage—accommodating the Bible's language to the people's current knowledge of nature.

> [I]n order to adapt itself to the understanding of all people, it was appropriate for Scripture to say many things which are different from the absolute truth in appearance and in regard to the meaning of the words.[16]

If God had not accommodated himself to many of the Israelites' previous beliefs about nature, they may have rejected God's message entirely. If they were told, for example, that the earth moves, they would have questioned the human author's overall credibility. Jesus himself told Nicodemus, "If I told you earthly things and you do not believe, how will you believe if I tell you heavenly things?"[17] Of course, Jesus wasn't supporting his use of accommodation. Just the opposite—he was chastising Nicodemus for not believing the earthly things that *are* true.

But notice that the accommodation position—popular even among many theologians of the time—was extremely powerful. Any time a conflict between Scripture and "natural knowledge" confronts us, we can cheerfully acknowledge the discrepancy and chalk it up to Scripture obliging mankind's weakness. But the question is, *did* the biblical authors in fact accommodate the people's ignorance? Not everyone believed they did.

In any case, said Galileo, none of this should be troubling. Scripture isn't concerned with natural philosophy. Rather,

> the authority of the Holy Writ has merely the aim of persuading men of those articles and propositions which are necessary for their salvation and surpass all human reason, and so could not become credible through some other science or any other means except the mouth of the Holy Spirit itself.[18]

Now, there are times when the meaning of Scripture may be ambiguous. Galileo said, "It seems to me that in disputes about natural phenomena it [i.e., Scripture] should be reserved to the last place."[19] We should, that is, see what natural philosophy says about the technical workings of the cosmos and then interpret Scripture accordingly. And this was just what Castelli had said.

But, Galileo warned, if we proceed this way, we had better be very sure of our natural philosophy. And so it is good that Galileo had very high standards for natural philosophy. Following Aristotle, as we saw, he believed that science should be founded upon indubitable "sensory experience," and anything not directly observed should only be derived using strict logical proof, or "necessary demonstrations."[20]

With his *Letter to Castelli*, Galileo had taken the theological turn, and then only very reluctantly. But his hand had been forced.

18

WARNING SIGNS

G iven the seriousness of impending events, it was a good thing Galileo managed to have both his daughters enter a local convent. At the end of 1613 or the beginning of 1614, Virginia and Livia were admitted into the Monastery of Saint Matthew at Arcetri, a mile from Florence.[1] And though they were still too young to take vows, the abbess— a relative of Cosimo's secretary, Vinta—made sure they were fitted with dark brown habits.[2] Virginia would eventually take the name Sister Maria Celeste (appropriate, given her father's celestial discoveries), and Livia would become Sister Arcangela.[3] We know very little about Livia, other than she was melancholy and moody, perhaps as a result of the Spartan conditions of the convent.

In December 1614, a Dominican, Tommaso Caccini—a colleague of Father Lorini's and associated with the anti-Galilean "Pigeon League"[4]—delivered a fiery sermon against Galileo and condemning Copernicanism. Playing off Galileo's name, Caccini began by quoting Acts: "Men of Galilee, why do

you stand looking at the sky?" The sermon text was—again—
Joshua 10. Caccini went so far as to say that mathematics is a
diabolical art and that all mathematicians should be run out of
Italy.[5] But the Dominicans disapproved of Brother Caccini's
tactics, and in January 1615, Galileo received an official apol-
ogy from a Dominican preacher-general in Rome.[6] It turned
out that Caccini had a reputation for tactless and overzealous
sermons.

Galileo also received assurance from a close friend in Rome,
Father Giovanni Ciampoli, that Caccini's sermon was of no real
consequence. Nevertheless, Ciampoli advised Galileo not to
venture into theology but to stick to mathematics.[7] Ciampoli had
spoken with Maffeo Barberini, Galileo's friend from Cosimo's
dinner party:

> Cardinal Barberini, who as you know from experience, has
> always admired your talents, told me only yesterday evening
> that with respect to these opinions he would like greater cau-
> tion in not going beyond the arguments used by Ptolemy and
> Copernicus, and finally in not exceeding the bounds of phys-
> ics and mathematics. For to explain the Scriptures is claimed
> by theologians as their field, and if new things are brought in,
> even though to be admired for their ingenuity, not everyone has
> the dispassionate faculty of taking them just as they are said.[8]

This division of knowledge into matters of faith and matters of
science was commonplace. But given Galileo's future dealings
with Barberini, it is an important report.

Father Lorini saw Galileo's *Letter to Castelli* and, in February 1615, sent a copy of it to the Holy Office of the Inquisition in Rome. Lorini complained that the "Galileists" follow Copernicus and that Galileo's letter "contains many propositions that seem either suspect or rash."[9] He continued, "Moreover, I hear . . . that they trample underfoot all of Aristotle's philosophy, which is so useful to scholastic theology."[10] Nevertheless, he said, "I declare that I regard all those who are called Galileists as men of goodwill and good Christians, but a little conceited and fixed in their opinions."[11] Lorini's letter marks the beginning of the Inquisition's official interest in Copernicanism, and the Holy Office asked its Florentine branch for the original letter to Castelli.[12]

When Galileo heard that Father Lorini had sent a copy of his *Letter to Castelli* to the Inquisition, he sent his own copy to a friend in Rome, Monsignor Piero Dini. Galileo wanted to make sure that the letter the authorities saw had not been altered. Galileo asked Dini to give a copy to a Jesuit mathematician and, if possible, to Cardinal Bellarmine himself. Galileo was confident that the Jesuits would agree with his views on Scripture and "natural knowledge."[13]

Dini wrote back that he had spoken to Cardinal Bellarmine on the Copernican issue and that "the Most Illustrious Bellarmine"

assured me he has not heard anyone talk about [the thing you mention] at all, ever since he discussed them orally with you. In regard to Copernicus, His Most Illustrious Lordship says he cannot believe that it is about to be prohibited;

rather, in his view, the worst that could happen to the book is to have a note added to the effect that its doctrine is put forth in order to save the appearances.[14]

So there *was* talk of Copernicus's *De Revolutionibus*. But as long as the motion of the earth was considered merely a calculational device and not as a thesis about the actual workings of the universe, there shouldn't be a problem. But that was just it: Galileo took Copernicanism as genuinely true, not merely as a mathematical tool. Now that theologians were getting involved, the stakes were rising.

In March, the bombastic Father Caccini arrived in Rome to take office at the Dominican monastery of the Minerva. He also took the opportunity to meet with a fellow Dominican who was a member of the Inquisition. Caccini expressed his concern over Galileo's views (although acknowledging that many people regarded Galileo as "a good Catholic").[15] The next day, the Inquisition granted Caccini a hearing. The following is part of his statement:

I declare to this Holy Office [of the Inquisition] that it is a widespread opinion that the above-mentioned Galiliei holds these two propositions: the earth moves as a whole as well as with diurnal [daily] motion; the sun is motionless. These are propositions which, according to my conscience and understanding are repugnant to the divine Scripture expounded by the Holy Fathers.[16]

After its investigation, the Holy Office concluded that Caccini was right to be concerned about Galileo's Copernicanism.[17] Galileo and Copernicanism both needed to be watched.

≈

But some clergy were in favor of Copernicanism. In January 1615, a well-respected Carmelite friar, Antonio Foscarini, had published a *Letter on the Pythagorean and Copernican Opinion of the Earth's Motion and Sun's Rest and on the New Pythagorean World System*, arguing that the Copernican view was compatible with Scripture. Foscarini had sent his book to Cardinal Bellarmine for his official opinion. Bellarmine replied to Foscarini in April, at first repeating what he had told Dini, that Copernicanism is a fine mathematical tool. But he continued with what can hardly be described as anything but a warning:

> However, it is different to want to affirm that in reality the sun is at the center of the world . . . this is a very dangerous thing, likely not only to irritate all scholastic philosophers and theologians, but also to harm the Holy Faith by rendering Holy Scripture false.[18]

In other words, when Scripture speaks of the sun's motion, it is speaking the literal truth; it isn't accommodating or speaking figuratively. And so to say that the sun is stationary would be to imply that Scripture is genuinely wrong on that issue. Bellarmine's example was from Psalm 19:

WARNING SIGNS | 121

> In [the heavens] He has placed a tent for the sun,
> Which is as a bridegroom coming out of his chamber;
> It rejoices as a strong man to run his course.
> Its rising is from one end of the heavens,
> And its circuit to the other end of them.[19]

This, it is important to remember, was the opinion of the Catholic Church's leading theologian.

Bellarmine went on to discuss the Council of Trent's ruling on the interpretation of Scripture, reminding Foscarini that "the Council prohibits interpreting Scripture against the common consensus of the Holy Fathers."[20] The Council of Trent, in 1546, decreed:

> In matters of faith and moral pertaining to the edification
> of Christian doctrine, no one relying on his own judgment
> and distorting the Sacred Scriptures according to his own
> conception shall dare to interpret them contrary to that sense
> which Holy Mother Church, to whom it belongs to judge of
> their true sense and meaning, has held or does hold, or even
> [to interpret them] contrary to the unanimous agreement of
> the Fathers.[21]

Notice that the Council limited the subject matter to "faith and morals." Foscarini was, of course, familiar with this caveat, but like Galileo, he believed that Copernicanism was neither a matter of faith nor morals.

But Bellarmine disagreed. The alleged motion of the earth is a matter of faith in the sense that to deny it would be to deny what the Holy Spirit claims. Just as it would be heretical to say "that Christ was not born of a virgin," it would be similarly heretical to say "that Abraham did not have two children or Jacob twelve."[22] To say either would imply that the Holy Spirit had lied.

In this way, everything in Scripture becomes a matter of faith, and so Bellarmine was going far beyond Trent. But this was the Counter-Reformation—life in wartime—and Bellarmine was shoring up the defenses.

Furthermore, Bellarmine said, with respect to the "unanimous agreement of the Fathers," (the Council of Trent's phrase) "you will find all agreeing in the literal interpretation that the sun . . . turns around the earth at a great speed, and that the earth . . . sits motionless at the center of the world."[23]

Yet Bellarmine did not rule out the possibility that someday it might be "demonstrated" that the sun is the center of the cosmos. If this did occur, then it would certainly be necessary to modify "with great care" our understanding of the relevant passages. Nevertheless, he confessed that he had "very great doubts" that such a demonstration would be found, and in any case, he said, "I will not believe that there is such a demonstration, until it is shown to me."[24] Reasonable enough. And Bellarmine was certainly right that there was as yet no *demonstration* of Copernicanism. Proving Copernicanism using the axiomatic method was simply too high a standard.

19

THE CRUX

Galileo saw Bellarmine's response to Foscarini and saw potential trouble. Philosophical conflict was one thing, theological conflict quite another. His own *Letter to Castelli* had been hastily written. He needed to take more care spelling out his views on the relation between natural knowledge and the Bible. So in 1615, Galileo reworked and expanded the *Letter to Castelli*, the result being his famous *Letter to the Grand Duchess Christina*. The grand duchess was an obvious choice as the official recipient; she, after all, had prompted the original discussion with Castelli.

Even as an unpublished letter, it was dangerous. In effect, wherever Galileo disagreed with Bellarmine, he would be challenging the Catholic Church's foremost theologian, one who was a member of the Roman Inquisition. And as a philosopher, this simply wasn't Galileo's place. The Council of Trent had made that clear. But Galileo had an irrepressible optimism regarding the reasonableness of Church officials, an optimism that bordered on naiveté. Throughout his life Galileo seemed oblivious to the Catholic Church's embattled position, trusting in calm, cool reason to win the day. And much of this optimism may have been due to a belief that God himself would make sure that truth prevailed.[1]

Bellarmine, recall, had warned Foscarini that "the Council prohibits interpreting Scripture against the common consensus of the Holy Fathers."[2] In the *Letter to Castelli*, Galileo hadn't taken the time to appeal to the Church Fathers' authority. He would not make that mistake again. Galileo peppered his letter to Christina with quotes from St. Augustine's *On the Literal Interpretation of Genesis*, a work in which Augustine had dealt with issues similar to those encountering Galileo. Christians—Catholics and Protestants—held Augustine in very high regard.

As before, Galileo pointed out that the proper interpretation of Scripture cannot conflict with the proper interpretation of nature. He also reiterated that the Bible's purpose is to teach salvation, not science. Galileo approvingly quoted Cardinal Cesare Baronio: "The intention of the Holy Spirit is to teach us how one goes to heaven and not how heaven goes."[3] It shouldn't, therefore, surprise us when Scripture speaks figuratively or accommodates its language to the views of its original recipients. Even the great Augustine suggested that the Creation "days" be taken metaphorically.[4]

≈

The issue here—in fact, the crux of the entire Galileo affair—can be boiled down to the interpretation of texts. In this case, the two texts are Scripture and the book of nature. In 1605, Francis Bacon had famously said that God gave us two books to study: his world and his Word. Because God is the author of both books, they can never—when properly interpreted—conflict. Bellarmine and Galileo agreed entirely on this crucial point. And on others as well. As Thomas Dixon explains:

> On all sides of the Galileo case there was agreement that it was proper and rational both to seek accurate knowledge of the world through observations of nature and also to base one's beliefs on the Bible. The conflict was not between empirical science and authoritarian religion but rather between differing views within the Catholic Church about how to interpret nature and Scripture, especially when they seemed to disagree.[5]

Problems only arise, therefore, when the two books seem to conflict. Navigating such conflicts requires careful consideration of how we interpret each book.

In general, the default interpretation of Scripture is the literal one, but when the literal interpretation conflicts with something we think we've discovered about nature, what then? Galileo approvingly quoted Augustine:

> There should be no doubt about the following: whenever the experts of this world [i.e., natural philosophers] can truly demonstrate something about natural phenomena, we [i.e., theologians] should show it not to be contrary to our Scriptures.[6]

Suppose that natural philosophers possess—in Galileo's terms—
"clear observations or necessary demonstrations" for some scientific claim, a claim that seems to conflict with Scripture. In
such an instance, theologians should show how Scripture can be
reconciled with science (again, maybe the Bible is speaking figuratively or simply accommodating the people's current views of
the cosmos).

But, on the other hand, if natural philosophers *don't* have
clear observations (from sense perception) or necessary demonstrations (from reason), then theologians should show by
any means possible that the science is false.[7]

All of this aligns perfectly with Bellarmine's position. But in
the *Letter to the Grand Duchess Christina*, Galileo was sometimes
ambiguous. There are places where he seems to give a rather different view. Because Scripture doesn't intend to teach natural
philosophy, it seems we need not even try to reconcile the book
of nature with Scripture. The two books are interested in entirely
different things. Therefore, if the biblical authors speak figuratively or accommodate the people's understanding of the world,
we can ignore any apparent conflict with science. The Bible isn't
teaching these things; it is merely using them as a means to con-
vey the message of salvation. This is, in essence, the Catholic
Church's position today.[8]

Near the end of his *Letter to the Grand Duchess Christina*,
Galileo repeated a point he made to Castelli about the danger of
the Church making rash pronouncements about science. Such
premature declarations could, he pointed out, seriously hurt the
Church's witness to the unbelieving world. If the evidence for

a scientific position is strong enough, then we might cause un-
believers to question the reliability of the Christian Scriptures.
This time, Galileo quoted Augustine:

> The distressing thing is not so much that an erring man [i.e.,
> the believer] should be laughed at, but that our authors [of
> Scripture] should be thought by outsiders to believe such
> things, and should be criticized and rejected as ignorant,
> to the great detriment of those whose salvation we care
> about. For how can they believe our books in regard to the
> resurrection of the dead, the hope of eternal life, and the
> kingdom of heaven, when they catch a Christian commit-
> ting an error about something they know very well, when
> they declare false his opinion taken from those books, and
> when they find these full of fallacies in regard to things
> they have already been able to observe or to establish by un-
> questionable argument?[9]

Galileo, however, was careful to explain that he was concerned that theologians would condemn Copernicanism before
philosophers gave it its day in court. "I propose not that this book
[Copernicus's *De Revolutionibus*] should not be condemned, but
that it should not be condemned without understanding, examin-
ing, or even seeing it."[10] But of course, Galileo firmly believed
that if Copernicus's views were carefully considered, they would
not be condemned. In any case, he hoped that the Copernican
issue would remain open long enough for it to be carefully and
freely discussed.[11]

Galileo also wanted the philosophers to remember their place. He was quick to point out that they had no authority when it comes to the ecclesiastical condemnation of scientific views. Leave theology to the theologians where it belongs:

> Thus let these people [i.e., philosophers] apply themselves to refuting the arguments of Copernicus and of the others, and let them leave its condemnation as erroneous and heretical to the proper authorities; but let them not hope that the very cautious and very wise Fathers and the Infallible One with his absolute wisdom are about to make rash decisions like those into which they would be rushed by their special interests and feelings.[12]

The Copernican view should be judged on scientific grounds. Galileo seemed confident that he had—or would soon have—the "clear observations or necessary demonstrations." He was wrong.

20

COPERNICUS MAKES
THE LIST

G iven the Inquisition's recent interest in Galileo (thanks to the Dominicans Caccini and Lorini), Galileo felt that it was time to make another appearance in Rome to defend himself. A trip to the Eternal City would also allow him to make the best possible scientific case for Copernicanism. Perhaps he could prevent Church officials from hastily condemning the view.

In November 1615, the Grand Duke Cosimo informed the Tuscan ambassador in Rome, Piero Guicciaridini, that he had gladly granted Galileo's request "to defend himself against the accusations of his rivals." The grand duke also ordered that Galileo be given two rooms in the Villa Medici because "he needed peace and quiet on account of his poor health."[1] Galileo arrived in Rome in December and immediately began making his rounds with the Roman officials.

Throughout his trip Galileo conscientiously kept the grand duke informed of his affairs. In these letters he frequently mentioned his reputation. But Galileo wasn't concerned primarily with his reputation as a mathematician or philosopher. Rather, as William Shea—who holds the Galileo Chair of the History of Science at the University of Padua—said:

> From his letters, it is clear that he was intent on defending himself from the insinuation that he was a masked heretic when he believed himself to be a good Catholic and an obedient son of the Church. This was not merely a political move. It expressed the ideal of a Christian scientist that had matured in his mind and that he saw himself as embodying. He may have been arrogant and naïve; he was not being dishonest.[2]

Galileo saw himself as a new kind of Christian natural philosopher, one who eschewed rigid appeal to pagan philosophers (like Aristotle). Later in the century, Isaac Newton, Robert Boyle, and others involved in England's Royal Society would see themselves similarly. These scientists—often called *virtuosi*—saw science as a natural outworking of a Christian desire to know God and his creation.

Galileo, therefore, criticized the Aristotelians for a *misplaced* faith.[3] To his mind, only the Church could command such an allegiance, and certainly not a heathen philosopher.

Soon, Galileo wrote back to Florence that "his reputation was growing every day." Even Caccini had paid him a humble and apologetic visit.[4] Now Galileo could take time to address the Copernican issue, despite the Tuscan ambassador's warning that Galileo should drop the subject, given the political climate in Rome. "This is no place," said the ambassador, "to come and argue about the Moon."[5]

＝

The grand duke had recommended Galileo to his cousin, Allessandro Orsini. Orsini, despite being only twenty-two, had recently been made a cardinal.[6] With the grand duke's endorsement in hand, Galileo asked Cardinal Orsini to speak to the pope about Copernicanism. The young cardinal readily agreed.

Galileo knew that if he was going to convince theologians to reinterpret biblical passages like Joshua 10, he needed a compelling argument for Copernicanism, one based on "clear observation and necessary demonstration." Any proof would therefore have to be by way of demonstration and not clear observation, since we certainly don't *see* the earth move. Rather, we *reason* to the earth's motion. Notice that the "text" of nature—the direct observations—were identical for both Galileo and the Aristotelians. It was just that Galileo differed on the *interpretation* of the observations.

But both sides agreed that the standards for reason were high—namely, rigorous "demonstration" or "proof." And about twenty years earlier Galileo had struck upon just such a proof (he believed), and now he was ready to deploy it. In January 1616, Galileo wrote out this argument for Orsini in a letter entitled *Discourse on the ebb and flow of the tides*.[7] Galileo argued in the letter that the earth's *diurnal* (daily) rotation and its yearly revolution caused the seas' oscillating tides.

The following month Orsini presented Galileo's argument to Pope Paul V. Things went about as poorly as they could have, as the Tuscan ambassador later explained:

> The Pope told [Orsini] it would be well if he persuaded [Galileo] to give up that opinion. Thereupon Orsini replied something urging the cause, and the Pope cut him short and told him he would refer the business to the Holy Office [of the Inquisition]. As soon as Orsini had left, his Holiness summoned Bellarmine; and after discussing the matter, they decided that the opinion was erroneous and heretical.[8]

This was exactly the opposite of what Galileo had hoped for. Instead of persuading the pope to protect Copernicanism, the meeting had set the Inquisition in motion against it. And maybe against Galileo.

On February 19, 1616, at the behest of the pope, the Holy Office of the Inquisition asked a panel of eleven theologians to judge the following Copernican theses:[9]

> The Sun is the center of the world and hence immovable of local motion.
>
> The Earth is not the center of the world, nor immovable but moves according to the whole of itself, also with a diurnal motion.

The panel of "consultors" was to weigh the scientific evidence, to see whether the evidence was strong enough to count as "demonstration." Although the members of the panel were certainly experts in theology, they knew neither science nor mathematics.[10] Yet within a week—an extremely short time for such a matter[11]—the panel returned their decision.

The panel declared that the first thesis, regarding the immobility of the sun, was

> foolish and absurd in philosophy, and formally heretical, inasmuch as it expressly contradicts the doctrine of the Holy Scripture in many passages, both in their literal meaning and according to the general interpretation of the Fathers and Doctors.[12]

In other words, the consultors considered the scientific (philosophical) evidence so paltry that belief in a stationary sun was not merely wrong but "foolish and absurd." This meant that there was no good reason to overthrow the standard interpretations of passages such as found in Joshua. In fact, the belief in an immovable sun was "formally heretical." And perhaps even impolite.

The panel similarly judged the second thesis regarding the earth's motion, although it didn't go so far as to call it heretical. It was, rather, "to receive the same censure in philosophy and, as regards theological truth, to be at least erroneous in faith."[13] So it, too, was "foolish and absurd" as a scientific claim. And although a Catholic could, strictly speaking, believe that the earth moves, such a view was incorrect as far as theology was concerned. But it was not heretical.

⁓

Officially, the consultors could only recommend their decision, but the Inquisition immediately accepted it. And because Galileo was closely associated with the controversy, the pope ordered his personal theologian, Cardinal Bellarmine, to meet with Galileo privately, to inform him of the Inquisition's position (although the Holy Office would publish their decision for all Catholics to see). Bellarmine's meeting with Galileo was private in order to avoid humiliating the grand duke.[14] But if Galileo balked at the Inquisition's decision, said the pope, he was to be given an official order before a notary and witness. This would raise the stakes: if Galileo remained obstinate, he was to be imprisoned.[15]

The details of this important meeting are unclear, but we know that Galileo immediately accepted the Inquisition's decree. Bellarmine then, to make things proper, gave Galileo a letter clearly stating that he might not defend or even *hold* Copernicanism. This, however, left open the possibility that—as Bellarmine had indicated in his letter to Foscarini—Copernicanism could be used as a fictional calculating tool.[16] And in theory, Catholics could discuss Copernicanism, as long as they didn't actually endorse it.

In March, the issue moved from the Inquisition to the Congregation of the Index, the body that determined which works were put on the *Index of Prohibited Books*. The Congregation was comprised of a handful of cardinals, including Bellarmine and Galileo's friend, Cardinal Barberini. The Congregation gave their recommendation to the pope, and on March 5, 1616, their historic decree was published.[17]

The Congregation ruled that Copernicus's *De Revolutionibus* was to be suspended until the proper corrections were made, and Foscarini's book was condemned outright.

But the Congregation had viewed the Inquisition's term "heretical" as too strong. Although the pope had wanted the Congregation to declare the book formally heretical, two of the Congregation's members objected, and "the Pope was stopped right at the beginning."[18] One of the opposing cardinals was Cardinal Barberini. Years later, a Galilean supporter told Barberini (who by then had become Pope Urban VIII) of some German Protestants who had almost converted to Catholicism but changed their minds upon hearing the Congregation's decision. When the pope heard this, he winced, replying, "This was never our intention, and if it had been left to us, that Decree would not have been made."[19]

Copernicus's *De Revolutionibus* was now on the *Index* but, technically, Catholics could read it, once a number of emendations were made. Moreover, very few actual corrections were required, and these amounted mostly to crossing out the rare passage in which the earth was said to move.[20] The Congregation, however, didn't publish the list of corrections until 1620.

Thankfully—for Galileo and the grand duke—Galileo's name had been left out of the decree. Nevertheless, Galileo was in a dangerous position. *De Revolutionibus* was put on the *Index* just when Galileo was publicly defending it. He was now associated with a theory the Inquisition had condemned.

And so Galileo asked Tuscany for a recommendation to meet with the pope, and on March 12 Pope Paul V gave Galileo an audience.[21] Galileo did not try to convince the pope to change the Inquisition's or the Congregation's verdicts. He merely wanted to assure the pope that he had every intention of complying with both, and that he was worried about "the malice of his persecutors" (he probably had Caccini and Lorini in mind). Galileo reported back to Tuscany with good news:

> [The pope] answered that he was well aware of my uprightness and sincerity and, when I showed signs of being still somewhat anxious about the future because of the fear of being pursued with implacable hate by my enemies, he cheered me up and said that I could put all care away because I was held in such esteem by himself and the whole Congregation that they would not lightly lend their ears to calumnious reports, and that I could feel safe as long as he was alive.[22]

Nevertheless, rumors spread through Italy that the Inquisition had summoned Galileo to Rome and charged him with heresy. Such gossip was bad for the grand duke's reputation, as well as Galileo's. So in May, Galileo appealed to Cardinal Bellarmine, who gave him a written affidavit fully exonerating him.[23]

The whole thing had gotten entirely out of hand. It was time for Galileo to leave Rome before something worse happened. He returned to Florence in June 1616.

㉑

ESCAPING THE
LABYRINTH

Galileo could discuss Copernicanism without endorsing it, but the issue was entirely too hot, and he had only *just* avoided serious trouble. Better to let things cool down; there was always hope that the Catholic Church's position on Copernicus would change. In the past there had been other books that—after being placed on the *Index* under one pope— had been removed by the next. In fact, years before, one of Cardinal Bellarmine's own books—in which he had limited the earthly power of the papacy—temporarily made the list. Waiting was the best thing Galileo could do.

So he turned to other things. He worked on a method for the particularly recalcitrant problem of determining longitude at sea (a method that relied on observing the satellites of Jupiter). He also began to rework his studies on motion, probably intending to publish them. But Galileo's efforts were constantly interrupted by his recurring illness. In 1617, he and Vincenzio finally moved to a villa in Bellosguardo, just outside Florence.[1]

In November 1618, Galileo was sick in bed when three comets appeared, inciting the usual concern over imminent plague, war, or apocalypse (incidentally, the Thirty Years' War began almost immediately). The Jesuit mathematician Orazio Grassi at the Collegio Romano, who now held Christopher Clavius's position (Clavius had died in 1612), gave a lecture on the physical nature of the comets. And rather than follow Aristotle, Grassi claimed that the comets were beyond the moon's sphere and therefore not in the terrestrial realm.

Galileo heard of the published account of Grassi's lecture in March 1619. There was also talk that the lecture refuted Copernicanism. Galileo couldn't address that, of course, but he could still undermine the lecture as a whole, by refuting Grassi's position on the comets. Ironically, Galileo believed, with most Aristotelians, that comets might be located *within* the moon's orbit, perhaps caused by the earth's atmosphere.[2] But he wasn't sure. In fact, Galileo's real point in his debate with Grassi would be that more evidence was needed before any pronouncements could be made about the nature of comets. Grassi's declaration was premature.

Galileo's planned refutation would be his first major work since the condemnation of 1616; it was therefore important that he take care and strike the right tone. His thoroughness slowed his work to a crawl.

~

Marina Gamba, Galileo's former lover and the mother of his children, had died in February 1619. In June, Galileo asked

Cosimo to clean up some of the family mess by legitimizing Vincenzio, then twelve years old. But there were other family difficulties. Galileo's mother, Giulia, was now in her eighties, and old age had done nothing to improve her temper. Galileo's brother, Michelangelo, wrote to Galileo with the following consolation: "But she is much aged, and soon there will be an end to all this quarreling." Michelangelo lived in Germany, his own consolation.[3] Giulia died the next year.

The following year—1621—the Grand Duke Cosimo died unexpectedly at the age of thirty. His oldest son, Ferdinando II, was only eleven years old, so his mother, Maria Magdalena of Austria, and his grandmother, Grand Duchess Christina, ruled Tuscany until he reached his majority. Cosimo's protection through the years had kept Galileo relatively safe; it had been suggested that it was because of the grand duke that Galileo had not stood trial when Copernicanism was condemned in 1616. Even after Ferdinando turned eighteen, he would not be able to provide the protection that Galileo needed. But perhaps no one could.

There were more deaths that year. The two men who had been most influential in Copernicanism's condemnation also died. In fact, they were the two most powerful men in the Catholic Church. Pope Paul V died of a stroke in January, and Cardinal Bellarmine (who had recently written *The Art of Dying Well*) died that fall.

Galileo wasn't doing so well either. He fell ill yet again early that year and was unable to write. This further postponed his response to Grassi's lecture on the comets. But by midyear he had recovered, and he threw himself back into his work.

By the fall of 1622, Galileo finished his response. He called it *Il Saggiatore*, or *The Assayer*, indicating that he would *weigh* Grassi's arguments in the balance.[4] Archimedes would no doubt approve of the title. But when Grassi later responded to *The Assayer*, instead of referring to it as *Il Saggiatore*, he called it *Assagiatore*, which means "winetaster," the point being that Galileo had been drinking when he wrote it.[5]

Galileo's book is, by all accounts, a marvel of polemics and Italian prose.[6] Its stated topic was the comets of 1618. But throughout the work, Galileo addressed a much broader topic: his proposed method of science. One of the reasons Copernicanism was condemned was due to its alleged lack of philosophical (scientific) support. But with a proper scientific method, Galileo believed, the evidence for Copernicanism would eventually become just that: *evident*. In this way, Galileo could support Copernicanism without mentioning it.

In *The Assayer*, Galileo contrasted his own mathematical science with Aristotle's reliance on obscure semantic and logical distinctions. Moreover, Renaissance science had degenerated into a futile game of interpreting Aristotle's texts. If there is any text that natural philosophers should read, believed Galileo, it is the Book of Nature. In one of history's most famous statements on the new method, Galileo chastised those who believe that

> in philosophizing one must rely upon the opinions of some famous author, so that if our mind does not marry the thinking of someone else, it remains altogether sterile and

fruitless. Perhaps he thinks that philosophy is the creation of a man, a book like the *Iliad* or *Orlando Furioso*, in which the least important thing is whether what is written in them is true . . . [T]hat is not the way it is. Philosophy is written in this all-encompassing book that is constantly open before our eyes, that is the universe; but it cannot be understood unless one first learns to understand the language and knows the characters in which it is written. It is written in mathematical language, and its characters are triangles, circles, and other geometrical figures; without these it is humanly impossible to understand a word of it, and one wanders around pointlessly in a dark labyrinth.[7]

The problem, then, was not so much that philosophers studied texts; it was that they studied the wrong texts. The proper text is the book of nature, whose author is divine. But without understanding its mathematical language, it is incomprehensible. If so, then Galileo implied—he did not come out and say this—that only mathematicians can read this text and are, therefore, the only ones who can pass judgment on its interpretations. Perhaps, however, his readers were also unable to read Galileo's subtext here.

The latter half of the quoted passage also marks the rebirth of the Pythagorean tradition. According to this ancient tradition, nature is fundamentally mathematical. Without such a belief, modern physics would be impossible. Indeed, scientists currently can't even *state* many of their theories without referring to mathematical entities like shapes, numbers, and functions.

Recall that Aristotelian science focused on nonmathematical qualities, like fast, slow, hot, and cold. Galileo's science, on the other hand, studied quantifiable properties: length, speed, acceleration, and time. Quantifiable properties are "mathematizable." But Galileo's science could not afford to ignore things like heat, and so heat, too, must become quantifiable. And it is here that Galileo employed an old Epicurean idea, one expounded by the first-century Roman philosopher Lucretius, in his poem *On the Nature of Things*.

In *The Assayer*, Galileo claimed that heat is not something that exists apart from our sense perception. That is, heat isn't in the fire but merely a sensation that occurs inside us.

> We have already seen that many properties, which are considered to be qualities inherent in external objects, do not really have any other existence except in us, and that outside of us they are nothing but names. Now I say that I am inclined to believe that heat is of this kind. The materials which produce heat in us and make us feel it, and which we call by the general name of *fire*, are large collections of tiny corpuscles shaped in such and such a manner and moving with such and such a speed . . . However, I do not believe in the least that besides shape, quantity, motion, penetration, and touch, there is in fire another quality, and that this quality is heat.[8]

The motion of atoms that make up the "hot" object cause the sensation of heat in us. These atoms or "corpuscles" do not

have a property called "heat," but only quantifiable properties, like size, shape, and speed. Nor do they have color, taste,
or smell. Those, too, are only sensations in us. "Thus," said
Galileo, "if living creatures were removed, all these qualities
would vanish and be annihilated."[9] Galileo reduced the study
of heat to the study of motion and other quantifiable aspects
of nature.

Notice also that these quantifiable properties are those that
cause *mechanical* phenomena in nature—those phenomena
that are caused by pushes and pulls.[10] A quantifiable universe
is a mechanical one, based on Archimedian simple machines.
According to Galileo's new natural philosophy, nature is
simultaneously mechanical and mathematical. This vision is
far more important than any of Galileo's physical discoveries
by themselves. The importance of Galileo's discoveries resides
in their support of his new science; they show that his vision
is possible.

In October 1622, Galileo sent a draft of *The Assayer* to
Prince Cesi's nephew, Duke Virginio Cesarini, also a member
of the Lyncean Academy in Rome.[11] It was Cesarini's job to
obtain the Church's *Imprimatur* for the book. Cesarini therefore
sent it to Niccolò Riccardia, a Dominican professor of theology
and consultor for the Holy Office of the Inquisition. Riccardi,
because of his "enormous girth, his weighty eloquence, and
his phenomenal memory,"[12] was called the "Father Monster."
In February 1623, the Father Monster not only approved *The
Assayer* but gushed over it. This would be important. Riccardi
would later be promoted to the Master of the Holy Palace, the

man who had final authorization of every work published in Rome.[13]

≈

In May 1623, Galileo's oldest sister, Virginia, died. But in this sad event, we have the first glimpse of Galileo's greatest joy: his twenty-two-year-old daughter, Virginia, now Sister Maria Celeste. In the first of more than a hundred letters from Maria Celeste to her father, she wrote:

> Most Illustrious Lord Father,
> We are terribly saddened by the death of your cherished sister, our dear aunt; but our sorrow at losing her is as nothing compared to our concern for your sake, because your suffering will be all the greater . . . Thus, for the love of God, we pray you, Sire, to be consoled and to put yourself in His hands, for, as you know so well, that is what He wants of you . . .
>
> Most affectionate daughter,
S. Maria Celeste[14]

We have none of Galileo's letters to her; they were destroyed soon after his trial in 1633. But his and Maria Celeste's relationship was undeniably close and affectionate. They spent much time together cooking and gardening and talking. Father Michael Sharratt says of Maria Celeste's letters:

> They are full of solicitude for his chronically precarious health; they are often accompanied by little presents

of home-made cakes, or clothes she had mended for him. Occasionally she makes requests for herself or her convent, requests which reveal both how poorly they lived and how little she looked for to keep her happy and supportive of others, especially her depressed sister. Now and again she proffers gentle spiritual advice, secure in the knowledge that it will not be taken amiss.[15]

When Galileo was old, blind, and under house arrest, Maria Celeste was his chief consolation.

NEW HOPE

I n August 1623, Galileo heard of a "wonderful juncture": his longtime friend, Cardinal Maffeo Barberini, had been elected Pope Urban VIII. It was simply too good to believe. Barberini not only respected Galileo; he had even written a Latin ode praising Galileo's scientific discoveries and marveling at the new world they revealed.

> When the moon shines and displays
> Its golden procession and its gleaning fires
> In its serene orbit
> A strange pleasure draws us and rivets our gaze.
> This one looks up at the shining evening star
> And the terrible star of Mars
> and the track colored with the luster of milk
> That one sees your light, O Cynosure.
> Or another marvels at either the heart of the Scorpio
> Or the torch of the Dog Star
> Or the satellites of Jupiter

> Or the ears of father Saturn
> Discovered by your glass, O learned Galileo . . .
> Not always, beyond the radiance that shines
> Does it become clear to us:
> We notice the black defects on the sun
> (Who would believe it?)
> By your art, Galileo.[1]

Barberini said that Galileo should accept the poem as a "small sign of the great good will that I have toward you."[2] And only a month before his election, Barberini had written Galileo:

> I remain much obliged to Your Lordship for your continued affection towards me and mine and I wish to have the opportunity to do likewise to you assuring you that you will find in me a very ready disposition to serve you out of respect for what you so merit and for the gratitude I owe you.[3]

And now Barberini was the head of the Catholic Church, sitting in the seat of the apostle Peter. Galileo—and the Lynceans—were clearly ecstatic. Maria Celeste wrote to Galileo of her "ineffable" happiness over Barberini's ascent to "Supreme Pontiff."[4]

Even better, two of Galileo's friends, Father Giovanni Ciampoli and Duke Virginio Cesarini (both Lynceans), obtained influential positions in the papal court—they were even placed high enough to directly influence Urban himself.[5] In a clever and strategic move, Cesarini read *The Assayer* to Urban during the pope's meals.[6] Urban was delighted by Galileo's views, as well as by his polemical prowess and beautiful Italian prose. And Urban no doubt also appreciated that *The Assayer* had been dedicated to him.

Galileo was now eager to make another trip to Rome, to congratulate his friend on his ascendency to the Church's highest earthly position. Unfortunately, his illness delayed him and it wasn't until April 1624 that he arrived in Rome. The day after his arrival, Galileo met with Pope Urban VIII for an hour. Urban immediately sent an official testimonial to the grand duke, expressing his affection for Galileo and admiration of his abilities.[7] Galileo's stock was quickly rising.

≈

During the next few months, Galileo met with Urban five more times, during which the two discussed Copernicanism. The pope viewed Copernicanism as a mathematical device that made no claim about the actual structure of the universe. But, Urban said, even if Copernicus had made such a claim, it would matter little. It was hubris to think that humans could say that God had necessarily made the universe in the way Copernicus—or anyone else—suggested. Urban's point was a theological one: Regardless of how nature appears to us, God is powerful enough to have made the underlying reality in a way incomprehensible to human minds. God could have used any number of means to produce the same appearances.[8] There was little Galileo could say to this. So he said nothing.

Nevertheless, Galileo proposed a project that the pope liked very much.[9] Galileo suggested he write a book showing that Italy still led the world in science and that the Church opposed Copernicanism only for theological reasons and out of scientific ignorance.[10] The 1616 edict had become unpopular among European intellectuals and was an obstacle to converts to Catholicism. This book could help change that.[11] The pope agreed, giving Galileo permission to write about Copernicanism as long as it was in a hypothetical way, as a mere calculational device to "save the phenomena."

Galileo returned to Florence in June 1624 with gifts from the pope: a painting, two medals, and several *Agni Dei* (wax discs with a seal of a lamb). Urban also promised to give Galileo's son, Vincenzio, an ecclesiastical pension.[12] According to the pension, Vincenzio would be made a canon of the Church, and therefore an official member of the clergy. The position was attached to a church in northern Italy, yet allowed Vincenzio to remain near Florence; the only real requirement was that he receive a tonsure to mark his entrance into the clerical state. (The tonsure was simply a small clipping of hair and not the shaved crown we associate with medieval monks.)[13] Vincenzio would then receive a small annual income for the rest of his life. It was easy work. Vincenzio rejected it anyway. He would try to find a government position, but eventually he became a chancellor of the Arte dei Mercatanti (the merchant's guild).[14]

Later, when another canonry opened at the cathedral in Pisa, Urban presented a second pension to Galileo himself, along with the customary reference to the new canon's "honest life and morals, as well as his other praiseworthy qualities of uprightness and virtue."[15] Galileo had his hair clipped and became a member of the clergy, which he remained the rest of his life.[16]

23

THE DIALOGUE

Back in Florence, Galileo immediately began writing his book on Copernicanism, which he referred to as "my dialogue on the tides" because his tidal theory was his main physical argument.[1] Authors frequently used dialogues for popular works; Galileo's father had used one years earlier. Dialogues allowed the author to clarify his views in response to a student's questions; it also put comfortable distance between him and controversial opinions.

Galileo's dialogue on the tides—written in Italian—took him more than five years to complete, because he was only able to write intermittently.[2] He suffered his usual bouts of illness—no less troublesome because of their familiarity; in fact, familiarity bred contempt. Galileo was in his sixties, and if statistics of the day were any indication, perhaps nearing the end of his life.

Yet he soldiered on, and by December 1629 his *Dialogue on the Tides* was nearly finished. It was time to wrap things up and take the book to Rome, where the Lynceans would publish it.

But illness struck again, and his trip to Rome was postponed. Galileo used this time—when he was up to it—to make additions and revisions to the *Dialogue*. This probably didn't speed his recovery, and Maria Celeste naturally worried that her father was overtaxing himself.[3]

By May 1630, however, Galileo's health had improved, and he left Florence with manuscript in hand. He arrived in Rome two days later, where his enemies made trouble almost immediately.

At the time, rumors were spreading that a horoscope cast by Father Orazio Morandi predicted the impending death of Urban and his nephew, Cardinal Francesco Barberini. Casting a horoscope of the pope and his family was officially illegal, and Urban—who was superstitious[4]—had Morandi imprisoned. But someone tried to connect Galileo with the crime, either as Morandi's friend or as the horoscope's actual author.[5] Galileo was understandably upset, but in June he received a comforting letter indicating that he had no better friend than the pope.[6] Not so with Morandi—within the year, he died awaiting trial.[7]

On December 18 Galileo had a friendly audience with the pope, but on the whole, Urban wasn't in the best of moods.[8] He had become increasingly troubled by the Thirty Years' War, which made him suspicious and irritable. He had little tolerance for disobedience, wherever he saw it (or even perceived it).[9]

The *Dialogue on the Tides* had been handed over to Riccardi, the Father Monster, who was now the Master of the Holy Palace. The reviewer—appointed by Riccardi—was a Dominican mathematics professor, Raffaele Visconti. Father Visconti soon discovered that the *Dialogue* favored Copernicanism (even if only as a mathematical tool) and recommended a number of corrections. Riccardi, too, required changes. He told Galileo to add an introduction and conclusion explicitly stating the hypothetical nature of Copernicanism.[10] Given Rome's political climate, Galileo should give no opportunity for misunderstanding.

When Riccardi reported to the pope that Galileo's book had been approved (subject to the recommended changes), the pope ordered that the title—*Dialogue of the Tides*—also be changed.[11] Having Copernicanism *explain* the tides suggested that Galileo was presenting it as the actual physical structure of the universe. But mathematical tools can't physically *cause* anything. And so, the official title became simply *Dialogue*.

This is not, however, the title by which we know the book. Since 1744, it's been called the *Dialogue Concerning the Two Chief World Systems—Ptolemaic and Copernican*, a phrase taken from a later subtitle.[12] Tycho Brahe's compromise system is conspicuously absent from the title, despite Brahe being a far stronger rival to Copernicus than Ptolemy.[13] Galileo has often been criticized for this omission, but Galileo in fact explicitly addressed the Tychonic system. And furthermore, because the tide argument is an argument for the earth's motion, if it is successful, then it works equally well against Brahe or Ptolemy, both of whom hold the earth stationary.

With the required changes, the *Dialogue* would officially conform to the Catholic Church's standards, including the edict of 1616. On June 16, 1630, Galileo received word that the *Dialogue* had been approved. Later that month, after receiving a warm farewell from Urban, Galileo returned to Florence to make the necessary revisions.[14] Once these were made, Galileo could send the book back to the Lynceans in Rome.

⁓

In August, however, the head of the Lynxes, Prince Cesi, died at the age of forty-five. He left no will and so left his affairs in chaos, chaos that spilled over into the Lyncean Academy. Now rudderless, the academy would soon come to an end.

The loss of a dear friend was bad enough for Galileo, but now the already bumpy process of getting the *Dialogue* published was even more difficult. Galileo himself would have to pilot the book through to the end.

But he couldn't very well travel to Rome. That summer the plague had entered Italy from the north and was spreading through the peninsula. In the 1300s, the plague's first European assault had begun in Italy, marching north. It killed a fourth of Europe. And here it was again, spreading panic along with death. The only way to slow the disease's spread was to isolate its human hosts; but quarantines slowed Italian daily life far more than they slowed the disease. The plague would remain for three years, killing one-third of Venice and half of Milan.[15]

Galileo was old, frail, and now surrounded by the plague. He couldn't afford to wait out the situation, and travel was nearly impossible for someone in his condition. Furthermore, even if Galileo survived the trip, the manuscript might not. In an attempt to prevent spreading infection, books were fumigated page by page, sprinkled with perfume, and their covers destroyed. Otherwise, they were burned entirely.[16]

Galileo, however, received permission to have the *Dialogue* printed in Florence. Unfortunately, the jurisdiction of Riccardi's permission to publish reached no farther than Rome's borders, so to print the book in Florence required another round of licensing. Riccardi, therefore, began sending instructions to the Inquisition censor in Florence.

The process dragged on for months, and the tedious back-and-forth between Florence and Rome made things nearly unbearable for Galileo. And even after the book received its second *Imprimatur*, printing took longer than expected. While he waited on the *Dialogue*, Galileo resumed his long-neglected work on motion.[17]

Around this time, Galileo's brother, Michelangelo, died in Munich. The friction between the brothers didn't remove the sting of death, and Maria Celeste became increasingly troubled by the toll taken on her sickly father. Moreover, Galileo began having problems with his eyes, at times severe enough to prevent him from reading and writing.[18] Maria Celeste recommended that her father move closer so she could care for him. She found a villa for rent in Arcetri, a house now called *Il Giollo*, "the jewel," a very short walk from the convent.[19]

Finally, on February 21, 1632, Galileo—now sixty-eight years old—received word that printing was complete and that the *Dialogue* would begin shipping immediately.[20] The grand duke received a presentation copy the next day.[21] The whole process had consumed nearly eight years of Galileo's life. But he hoped for a high yield on his investment, perhaps even a reversal of the 1616 decision against Copernicanism.[22]

≈

Galileo began the *Dialogue* with a preface "To the Discerning Reader," which immediately adds a personal touch, for every reader recognizes this as himself. In the preface, Galileo assuringly wrote that Copernicanism wasn't condemned because the Italians (and the Church) are ignorant of science and mathematics. Indeed, the erudite considerations contained in the book will show that Copernicus's views were rejected for admirable reasons.

> I hope from these considerations the world will come to know that if other nations have navigated more, we have not theorized less. It is not from failing to take count of what others have thought that we have yielded to asserting that the earth is motionless, and holding the contrary to be a mere mathematical caprice, but (if for nothing else) for those reasons that are supplied by piety, religion, the knowledge of Divine Omnipotence, and a consciousness of the limitations of the human mind.[23]

And the Catholic reasons for rejecting Copernicanism are the very ones that Urban repeatedly gave Galileo. Galileo, therefore, was making it very clear that, officially, he was in agreement.

The dialogue itself takes place among three men. One of the men, Filippo Salviati (named after Galileo's longtime friend who had died unexpectedly in 1614), is Galileo's main spokesman.

Galileo calls Salviati's Aristotelian opponent *Simplicio*, the Italian name for Simplicius, the ancient and esteemed commentator on Aristotle. Simplicio's arguments are based on those of Galileo's old Paduan friend, Cesare Cremonini, and on those of his Florentine enemy, Ludovico delle Colombe. The third man, a fence-sitter whose allegiance Simplicio and Salviati are each after, is Giovanfrancesco Sagredo, another old friend of Galileo's who had died in 1620. Unfortunately all three names begin with *s*, making it difficult at times, even for the discerning reader.

The *Dialogue*'s fictitious conversation takes place in Sagredo's Venetian palace over four days, a common way of breaking dialogues into chapters.[24] Each day is devoted to a different topic, each topic progressing logically toward the book's culmination—the tidal argument.

On the first day, Galileo—through Salviati—begins by undermining important Aristotelian principles. Most importantly, he attacks the terrestrial/celestial distinction. The moon's surface, the phases of Venus, sunspots, and the satellites of Jupiter should convince the Aristotelians that God fashioned the heavens out of the same material as ordinary terrestrial objects. Even Aristotle, Galileo says, would admit as much: "I declare that we do have in our age new events and observations such that if Aristotle were now alive, I have no doubt he would change his opinion."[25]

During the second day, the three men discuss the rotational motion of the earth. (They'll discuss the earth's annual path around the sun on day three.) The biggest problem for Copernicanism is this: it doesn't seem as if the earth is moving.

If our senses tell us anything, it's that the ground is absolutely still. Simplicio rightly points out that "in Copernicus's view one must deny one's own senses."[26] Simplicio could not be more right.

And Galileo agrees. The only thing he can say is that our senses are apparently wrong on this count. In fact, denying our senses can be a virtue.

> Nor can I ever sufficiently admire the outstanding acumen of those who have taken hold of this opinion and accepted it as true; they have through sheer force of intellect done such violence to their own senses as to prefer what reason told them over that which sensible experience plainly showed them to the contrary. For the arguments against the whirling of the earth which we have already examined are very plausible, as we have seen; and the fact that the Ptolemiacs and Aristotelians and all their disciples took them to be conclusive is indeed a strong argument of their effectiveness.[27]

This is an astonishing passage. Galileo—the man responsible for making observation and experiment a central part of science—cheerfully declares that the lack of observational evidence for a moving earth makes believing it all the more admirable.

But Copernicus didn't actually deny his observational evidence. Rather, he denied the natural *interpretation* of that evidence. Neither side of the debate disagrees about what we actually see and feel, but about what it *means*. The question is, what overall story best fits our observations?

Notice, then, what Galileo needs. To make Copernicanism plausible, he needs a new theory of terrestrial physics—a new theory of motion—one that can make sense of what Simplicio calls the "thousand inconveniences" of a moving earth. The earth's motion removes many of Aristotle's explanations of ordinary motion (like why objects fall to the ground). But Galileo's new terrestrial physics must do even more; it must also be applicable to the heavens. If there is no terrestrial/celestial distinction, there should, presumably, be only a *single set* of physical laws. Although Galileo would later publish his definitive work on motion (his "new science"), he addressed a few of the more salient issues in the *Dialogue*.

Imagine, for example, dropping a stone from a high tower. If the earth really does rotate, then the stone shouldn't land at the tower's base: while the stone falls, the earth has rotated slightly, presumably away from the stone.[28] But the stone *does* land at the tower's base, and this seems like a point in favor of a stationary earth. So Galileo must come up with a plausible story that accounts for the earth's rotation *and* the rock's behavior. His explanation is that the earth has imparted its own rotational motion to the stone, and when the stone is dropped, it keeps moving in the direction of that imparted motion. Galileo is altering his terrestrial physics to accommodate Copernicanism.

But there is another obvious objection to the earth's rotation. Why don't objects on the earth's surface fly off into space, like a rock from a sling? Galileo explains that it is because of an object's weight or *gravitas*.[29] Recall that Galileo had believed the Aristotelian view of heaviness or gravity: that an object's downward motion was caused by the object's internal nature that "desires" to reach its natural place of rest at the center of the cosmos. But now the earth is no longer at the center, so that explanation won't work.

Yet this is no real problem for Galileo—he no longer has any designs on the cause of fall. Who can say what the cause is? But whatever causes objects to fall to the earth, he thinks, also causes planets to remain in their orbits around the sun.[30]

Decades later Newton would echo this skepticism about the fundamental *causes* of phenomena when he "feign[ed] no hypotheses" about the cause of gravity. Newton wouldn't pretend to explain gravity, despite its clear effects. In fact, here is one of the most important rules of modern science: focus on descriptions of nature, not on fundamental explanations or causes. It is a fiercely anti-Aristotelian tenet.

On day three Galileo discusses the earth's annual trip around the sun. From our vantage on the earth, Mars, for example, sometimes reverses directions. This reversal is very difficult to explain if Mars is rotating around a stationary earth. However, if the earth is hurrying along with the planets around a stationary sun, we can easily account for this "retrograde" motion. When we overtake Mars during the planetary race, it looks as if it is moving backward; but when we move far enough away, Mars again looks as if it is moving forward. And this has a startling implication: the earth is a planet—a wandering star! And unlike Pluto, the earth will probably never be anything else.

The first three days were defensive, with Galileo addressing the main objections to a rotating and revolving earth. On day four, however, he goes on the offensive and offers what he considers positive support for Copernicanism: "If the Earth is at rest, the tides cannot occur, but if it moves with the motions described, they necessarily follow with all that is actually observed."[31] Although Galileo didn't present all the details in the *Dialogue*, he believed that the complete tidal argument provides a genuine *demonstration* for Copernicanism, and therefore it is strong enough to require a reinterpretation of passages like Joshua 10.

But no one believed him, and rightly so. For one thing, there was just too much evidence that the moon had something to do with the tides, something Galileo denied vigorously.[32] For another, there was no hint that Galileo *had* a demonstration. As Ernan McMullin points out, the fact that Galileo's central argument for Copernicanism had such serious problems made it all too easy for his opponents to dismiss the entire *Dialogue*.[33] And so they did.

≈

Even if the physical argument for Copernicanism was obviously unsuccessful, there was another, potentially more serious problem with it. Namely, it was a *physical* argument and not one suggesting that Copernicanism was merely a mathematical tool. So, to keep with the 1616 edict, Galileo closes with Urban's theological argument, namely, that regardless how good the physical explanation of the tides is, God could have always caused them in any number of ways.[34] At the very end of the fourth day's discussion, Simplicio repeats an argument that he heard from "a most eminent and learned person" (Pope Urban VIII), an argument before which "one must fall silent."

I know that if asked whether God in His infinite power and wisdom could have conferred upon the watery element its observed reciprocating motion using some other means than moving its containing vessels, both of you would reply that He could have, and that He would have known how to do this in many ways which are unthinkable to our minds. From this I forthwith conclude that, this being so, it would be excessive boldness for anyone to limit and restrict the Divine power and wisdom to some particular fancy of his own.[35]

Salviati (Galileo) concurs and adds:

An admirable and angelic doctrine, and well in accord with another one, also Divine, which, while it grants us the right to argue about the constitution of the universe (perhaps in order that the working of the human mind shall not be curtailed or made lazy) adds that we cannot discover the work of His hand.[36]

There is, Galileo's spokesman goes on to say, nothing wrong with these intellectual exercises, as long as we don't think that we've actually uncovered the reality behind the appearances.

Galileo intended the inclusion of Urban's argument to reduce any theory of the tides' cause—including Copernicanism—to an instrumental theory, one that may or may not be actually true. It doesn't rule out the possibility that Copernicanism is literally true, but it casts enough doubt on it to refrain from believing it. The *Dialogue*, therefore, ends in complete skepticism.

24

"AN OUTBURST OF RAGE"

Copies of the *Dialogue* were distributed throughout Europe. In Italy, however, the plague was making distribution difficult. In fact, the first copies to arrive in Rome were the eight that a friend of Galileo's had taken with him. But these eight were sufficient to get Rome talking about the *Dialogue*. And not all the talk was good.

In June 1632, Castelli wrote to Galileo of an incident in a Roman bookshop. A priest was praising the *Dialogue*, gushing that it was the greatest book ever printed. The Jesuit Christopher Scheiner—Galileo's old adversary from the sunspot controversy—was there. Scheiner was so upset by the priest's comments that he visibly shook, astonishing the shop owner. Scheiner then offered a huge price for an early copy of Galileo's book so that he could immediately refute it. When he finally did write his response, it was so violent that even his fellow Jesuits postponed its publication until after Scheiner's death in 1650.[1] An admirer of Galileo's wrote that Scheiner was distraught "because he would at all costs be the discoverer of

162

the [sun]spots."[2] Later, someone close to Cardinal Francesco Barberini's court would say, "All these storms are believed to be born of the hatred of one monk whom Galileo will not admit to be the greatest mathematician in the world."[3] Although we don't know exactly who is being spoken of here, some historians have naturally believed it to be Scheiner. In any case, Galileo would blame the Jesuits for his troubles, never the Church.[4]

Things got progressively worse. News of attempts to get the book condemned began to surface. The current Tuscan ambassador to Rome, Francesco Niccolini, reported that a hostile delegation had met with Cardinal Barberini, the pope's nephew.[5] But it wasn't until Urban VIII was finally informed of the *Dialogue*'s contents, that the firestorm erupted.

In July, the pope ordered the Master of the Holy Palace, Niccolò Riccardi (the Father Monster), to write the Florentine inquisitor, informing him that "Galileo's book has arrived and there are many things that are not acceptable and that the authorities want to see revised. The Sovereign Pontiff has ordered . . . that the book is to be withheld."[6] Urban then ordered a special Commission of Enquiry to investigate the *Dialogue*.

The problem, Riccardi reported, was threefold. First, the qualifying preface (to the "discerning reader"), which made plain that Copernicanism was only a mathematical tool, was printed in a different type, distancing its remarks from the dialogue itself. Second, according to the pope, Galileo had reduced the Supreme Pontiff's three theological arguments to one. And third, perhaps worst of all, Galileo put Urban's argument in the mouth of the debate's loser, Simplicio, "making it appear derided."[7] Not only that, in Italian *simplicio* can have the connotation of "simpleton."[8] Perhaps an enemy of Galileo's who was close to the pope had gingerly pointed this out to his Holiness. Galileo vigorously denied that he had intended any such thing, pleading with Cardinal Barberini to convince his uncle of his upright intentions. And it is true, both *simplicio* and *simplicius*, strictly speaking, mean "good" or "simple," as in "pure" or "without guile or deceit." Nevertheless, throughout the *Dialogue*'s discussion, Simplicio is cast in a less-than-favorable light; therefore, the pope reasoned, so was he.

Galileo should have been more careful. But again, he had always suffered from a good measure of political and rhetorical naiveté; add to that his frequent optimism about his opponent's ability to follow his arguments calmly and coolly, and we get the makings of a perfect storm. Perhaps if the pope had been able to emotionally distance himself, he would have seen—as Galileo and his friends pointed out—that Urban's theological argument couldn't have been reasonably put into the mouths of either of the *Dialogue*'s other two interlocutors. Maybe a calm, cool Urban would also have taken into account that Salviati himself endorsed Urban's argument, even strengthening it.

But Urban was unable to sufficiently disengage his emotions from his reason, something harder to do than most people think. And he was dealing with larger political issues—the Thirty Years' War and the ongoing Protestant "heresy," to mention only two—and his patience and tolerance were nearing their limits.

In September these limits were finally outstripped. Ambassador Niccolini had a meeting with the pope that went terribly wrong. When Niccolini brought up the subject of Galileo's book, the pope interrupted him "in an outburst of rage,"[9] exclaiming that Galileo had "entered on the most dangerous ground there was."[10] Galileo, Urban continued, should be happy that the Inquisition was not immediately brought in and that only a special commission was ordered. By this mercy, Urban said, he had treated Galileo better than Galileo had treated him. Furthermore, the pope warned, the grand duke had better not intervene, for there would be no way for him to "emerge with honor." Niccolini later reported that, from his own experience, "when his Holiness gets something in his head, that is the end of the matter, especially if someone tries to resist, oppose or defy him. Then he takes a hard line and shows no consideration whatsoever."[11]

Things were going as poorly as they could at this point. With the pope now against him, Galileo had little chance. James Reston says that "one remark by Pope Urban VIII explains the entire Galileo affair: 'He did not fear to make sport of me.'"[12]

≈

When the grand duke received word of the pope's reaction, he was furious.[13] How could a book that had been given the Church's *Imprimatur* be withheld? It is an imminently reasonable question. But apparently the *Imprimatur* did not absolve Galileo of his responsibility. Yet the real issue now was that the pope felt Galileo had deliberately deceived him; the *Dialogue* was nothing like what Urban had envisioned.

Surprisingly, Riccardi—the man who had given the *Dialogue* final approval—managed to keep his post as Master of the Holy

Palace; the pope believed that, like himself, the Father Monster had been deceived. But Father Giovanni Ciampoli, Galileo's friend and the person who had assured the pope that the contents of the *Dialogue* were acceptable, was exiled from Rome and placed in a menial position as the governor of a small village. He was never allowed to return to Rome.[14] Father Visconti, the Dominican mathematician who reviewed the *Dialogue* for Riccardi, was also sent into exile.[15]

The Commission of Enquiry recommended that Galileo's case be sent to the Inquisition. It was clear, the Commission said, that Galileo had argued too strongly for Copernicanism, despite his rhetorical flourishes to the contrary, thereby violating the 1616 edict against Copernicanism.

But something even more serious had recently come to light. In the Holy Office's files on the 1616 decree, an unsigned notary document was found (by whom we don't know). It was an account of the meeting between Cardinal Bellarmine and Galileo, the one in which Galileo was informed of the verdict against Copernicus. In itself, the meeting wasn't the problem. It was that, in addition to Bellarmine's warning to Galileo not to hold or defend Copernicanism (which applied to every Catholic), a Dominican commissary had further ordered Galileo not to teach or discuss Copernicanism in *any way whatsoever*. (The commissary had apparently ignored Pope Paul V's order to give Galileo this additional injunction *only if* he had balked at Bellarmine's warning.) Therefore, according to this document, Galileo couldn't discuss Copernicanism even as a mathematical tool. To make matters worse, Galileo had never mentioned a word of the meeting, much less the personal injunction that went beyond what generally applied to Catholics.

Urban was livid. Here was proof positive that Galileo had deliberately deceived him in order to get permission to write on Copernicanism. The pope (so he believed) had been betrayed— and by a man whom he trusted and respected.[16] Urban never allowed Galileo to speak to him personally again.[17] The only way Galileo could make sense of Urban's behavior was to blame it on the Jesuits' poisonous whispers.[18]

Unfortunately, the pope didn't know that Bellarmine had ordered Galileo to ignore the stronger injunction given by the commissary and that Pope Paul V had only asked Bellarmine to personally inform Galileo of the 1616 edict, not make further restrictions on him. Moreover, Bellarmine had told Galileo to act as if the commissary had never uttered the injunction.[19] And so Galileo had. Regrettably, the only witness to all this—Bellarmine himself—was dead.

~

On October 2, 1632, Galileo received orders to appear in Rome before the Inquisition to account for the *Dialogue*.[20] He was stunned. And he was gravely ill. He asked to be excused from traveling to Rome because of his poor health and old age.[21] Perhaps, Galileo suggested, he could present his defense in writing or deal with the Florentine inquisitors. But Urban was adamant: Galileo must appear before the Tribunal in Rome. In a show of what the pope must have considered extravagant grace, he allowed Galileo to delay his trip one month.

Galileo was still sick after the month. The Florentine inquisitor visited Galileo and reported to Rome that three physicians signed statements testifying that if Galileo were to travel, he might not survive the trip. The pope, however, believed that Galileo's illness was a subterfuge and informed him that he was to come to Rome at once, either of his own accord or in chains (and be charged the travel expenses of the arresting officers).

Galileo had a way out. William Shea explains, "Had Galileo been less devout, he could have refused to go to Rome; Venice offered him asylum."[22] But instead, Galileo left for Rome on January 20, 1633, on a litter provided by the grand duke. On the way, he was quarantined for two weeks, finally arriving in Rome on Februrary 13. The journey no doubt took its toll, but thankfully, Galileo was allowed to stay with Ambassador Niccolini at the Tuscan embassy rather than in the Holy Office's prison. The pope, however, made a point to say that this courtesy was a favor to the grand duke, not to Galileo.[23]

Despite the initial rush, the Holy Office waited two months before calling Galileo to his first hearing. The waiting and uncertainty took its toll on Galileo. This no doubt further upset Maria Celeste, who offered what comfort she could through prayers and weekly letters.

Finally, on April 12, 1633, Galileo—now sixty-nine—was moved from the Tuscan embassy to a comfortable apartment in the Holy Office's building with his attendant. That same day he appeared before the Tribunal of the Inquisition, a position considerably less comfortable than his lodgings.

25

VEHEMENT SUSPICION
OF HERESY

The Tribunal was not a court in our modern sense. The Inquisition had already judged Galileo guilty; it was now simply calling him to admit his guilt and to recant his errors. The only remaining legal issue was Galileo's sentence, and the Inquisition would decide that only after interrogations were complete.[1] Furthermore, we shouldn't imagine that the ten cardinals of the Inquisition were present during questioning; interrogations were left to a single prosecutor and his assistant. The cardinals would be told of the Tribunal's findings at their weekly meeting.

During the hearing Galileo acknowledged that Bellarmine had warned him not to hold or defend Copernicanism. Galileo then—and here he stunned the Tribunal—presented Bellarmine's affidavit of May 1616. The affidavit clearly states, explained Galileo, that "the opinion of Copernicus cannot be held or defended, because of its being against the Holy Scriptures."[2]

But, replied the prosecutor, what about the additional injunction "given in the presence of witnesses, namely that [you] might not *in any way* hold, defend or *teach* the said opinion?" Galileo responded that he didn't remember any prohibition on teaching; he had always relied on Bellarmine's affidavit, and it gave no such order.[3]

Keeping Bellarmine's affidavit probably saved Galileo from being burned at the stake. Here he had concrete evidence of Bellarmine's warning, one that was actually signed, unlike the recently uncovered notary's memorandum.

After some further questions, the Tribunal sent Galileo back to his quarters.

But even if Galileo had not gone so far as to outright disobey an injunction to not discuss (i.e., teach) Copernicanism, it still seemed that he had violated the edict of 1616. And, as Riccardi said, "this alone was sufficient to ruin him now."[4] And so Galileo was still guilty. But the Inquisition, probably under the advice of Cardinal Barberini, gave Galileo the opportunity to plea-bargain. Galileo was told that if he admitted to the lesser charge of defending Copernicanism, he would receive a more lenient sentence. Although not entirely comfortable with this concession—after all, he had not meant to outright defend Copernicanism— Galileo acquiesced. Perhaps, he mused, the *Dialogue*'s case for Copernicanism was too strong. Perhaps, indeed.

On April 20, 1633, Maria Celeste wrote to her father:

The only thing for you to do now is to keep your good

spirits, and take care not to jeopardize your health by wor-
rying too much. Direct your thoughts and hopes to God
who, like a tender, loving father, never abandons those who
confided in Him and appeal to Him for help in time of need.
Dearest father, I want to write to you now, to tell you that I
share your suffering in the hope of making it lighter for you
to bear. I have given no hint of these difficulties to anyone. I
keep the unpleasant news for myself and only mention what
you say is pleasant and satisfying. Thus we are all awaiting your return, eager to enjoy your delightful conversation
once again. And who knows, Sire, if while I sit writing, you
may not already find yourself released from your predica-
ment and free of all concerns? Thus may it please the Lord
Who must be the One to console you, and in Whose care I
leave you.[5]

Maria Celeste had heard of the events in Rome and was understandably distressed. She knew that, even under the best circumstances, her father was in poor health. And now his illness began
indirectly affecting her own health. If she wasn't careful, she
would worry herself to death.

Galileo was finally called to stand again before the Tribunal
on April 30. He confessed that, indeed, after going back through
the *Dialogue*, he had overstated the case for Copernicanism.
But, he added, this was entirely unintentional. In fact, he said,
"I inwardly and truly did and do hold them [the Copernican
arguments] to be inclusive and refutable." Unfortunately, he
admitted, he had succumbed to the

natural gratification everyone feels for his own subtleties and for showing himself to be cleverer than the average man, by finding ingenious and apparent considerations of probability even in favor of false propositions . . . My error then was, and I confess it, one of vain ambition, pure ignorance, and inadvertence.[6]

After his statement Galileo was allowed to return to the Tuscan embassy with Ambassador Niccolini. The cardinals of the Inquisition would be informed of his confession.

Some of the cardinals, however, doubted Galileo's sincerity. They consulted with the pope, who ordered that Galileo undergo an "examination of intention" in which Galileo would be further questioned while shown the instruments of torture. This was standard practice for both the Inquisition and nonecclesiastical courts of the day, although the Roman Inquisition rarely practiced torture.[7] Urban ordered that after Galileo's interrogation and threat of "rigorous examination"—a euphemism for torture[8]—he was to be imprisoned in Rome, subject to negotiations due to his plea bargain.[9]

On June 21, after two more unbearable months of waiting, Galileo had his third and final hearing. When asked, upon pain of torture, to state whether he had intended to defend Copernicanism, Galileo replied, "I am here to obey, and have not held [Copernicanism] after the determination [of 1616], as I said."[10] Thankfully, Galileo was not tortured, contrary to legend.[11] After the interrogation Galileo returned to the Tuscan embassy to await his sentencing the next day.

On June 22, Galileo was ordered to dress in the standard white penitential gown for sentencing. He was then led, on the mule of the Inquisition, to the Dominican convent of Saint Mary above Minerva, where he finally came face-to-face with the cardinals of the Inquisition.[12] Galileo knelt while his sentence was read:

> We [the Cardinals of the Holy Office] say, pronounce, sentence, and declare that you, the said Galileo, by reason of the matters adduced in trial, and by you confessed as above, have rendered yourself in the judgment of this Holy Office vehemently suspected of heresy, namely of having believed and held the doctrine which is false and contrary to the sacred and divine Scriptures . . . We condemn you to the formal prison of this Holy Office during our pleasure, and by way of salutary penance we enjoin that for three years to come you repeat once a week the seven penitential Psalms. Reserving to ourselves liberty to moderate, commute, or take off, in whole or in part the aforesaid penalties and penance.[13]

Three of the ten cardinals refused to sign the sentence—one of these was the pope's nephew, Cardinal Barberini. Drake points out that Galileo "was never without support among cardinals and other churchmen of high rank, who merely happened in the end to be outvoted."[14]

And though the pope was personally involved in the court's decision, the Holy Office's sentence wasn't officially "infallible."[15] Infallibility is only "invoked in special circumstances when an ecumenical council or the pope, acting as the head of the Church, solemnly defines a matter concerning faith or morals."[16] In other words, the sentence could be changed or rescinded.[17] For now, however, Galileo was to be imprisoned and the *Dialogue* placed on the *Index of Prohibited Books*.

The official verdict "vehemently suspected of heresy" was a less serious charge than "proven guilty of heresy." But notice that the Inquisition charged Galileo with actually believing Copernicanism. The Inquisition seems to not have taken seriously Galileo's claim to the contrary. And neither do many scholars. But there is strong evidence that, just as Galileo says in the *Dialogue*, he didn't believe that Copernicanism had been definitively proven. In 1641, as Drake points out, in "the last year of his life, with no hope of reward or any fear of further punishment,"[18] Galileo wrote:

> The falsity of the Copernican system must not on any account be doubted, especially by us Catholics, who have the irrefragable authority of Holy Scripture interpreted by the greatest masters in theology, whose agreement renders us certain of the stability of the earth and the mobility of the sun around it. The conjectures of Copernicus and his followers offered to the contrary are all removed by that most sound argument, taken from the omnipotence of God. He being able to do in many, or rather in infinite ways, that which to our view and observation seems to be done in one particular way, we must not pretend to hamper God's hand and tenaciously maintain that in which we may be mistaken.[19]

And Galileo correctly pointed out that this uncertainty doesn't apply to just Copernicanism:

> And just as I deem inadequate the Copernican observations and conjectures, so I judge equally, and more, fallacious and erroneous those of Ptolemy, Aristotle, and their followers, when [even] without going beyond the bounds of human reasoning their inconclusiveness can be very easily discovered.[20]

Galileo had written this in response to a claim that someone had "found conclusive evidence for the Copernican system."[21] Galileo was simply acknowledging a measure of uncertainty inherent in all scientific theories.[22] But, of course, Copernicanism is possible; it's just that "there is no event in Nature, not even the least that exists, such that it will ever be completely understood by theorists."[23] The high-octane Aristotelian standards for science cannot be met.

Galileo's famous abjuration came after the sentencing. Kneeling before the cardinals, Galileo read:

> I have been judged vehemently suspect of heresy, that is, of having held and believed that the Sun is the centre of the universe and immovable, and that the Earth is not the center of the same, and that it does move. Wishing, however, to remove from the minds of your Eminences and all faithful Christians this vehement suspicion reasonably conceived against me, I abjure with a sincere heart and unfeigned faith, I curse and detest the said errors and heresies, and generally

all and every error, heresy, and sect contrary to the Holy Catholic Church.[24]

Had Galileo refused to recant, the Inquisition would have upgraded the charge to "proven guilty of heresy" and burned Galileo at the stake, as had happened with Bruno. Moreover, once Galileo recanted, he was, in effect, silenced on Copernicanism forever; if he ever "relapsed" in any way, he would be burned alive.[25]

According to Galilean myth, after recanting Galileo defiantly uttered under his breath, *"Eppur si muove!"* ("And yet it moves!") This story, undeniably dramatic, is merely a projection of wish fulfillment by its authors.[26] It entirely misrepresents Galileo's attitude. Another legend—this one closer to the truth—has Galileo spending the rest of his life in an actual prison. Voltaire lamented,

> [T]he great Galileo, at the age of fourscore, groaned away his days in the dungeons of the Inquisition, because he had demonstrated by irrefragable proofs the motion of the earth.[27]

Although the official sentence indicated that Galileo was to be imprisoned, Galileo's sentence was—because of the plea bargain—immediately commuted to house arrest in the Villa Medici.[28] And though Ambassador Niccolini's attempt to convince the pope to pardon Galileo failed, Urban released Galileo into the custody of Archbishop Acanio Piccolomini in the Tuscan city of Siena, located thirty miles south of Florence.[29] Happily, the archbishop was a fervent admirer of Galileo. Just as the pope used to be.

Although Copernicanism was the centerpiece of both the 1616 edict and Galileo's trial in 1633, in terms of the Catholic Church's legal actions, the two cases were considerably different. In 1616, Rome pronounced against Copernicanism proper—in particular, against its main theses that the sun is the immovable center of the cosmos and that the earth moves around the sun. The Inquisition summoned Galileo, on the other hand, because of his alleged disobedience to an explicit Church order. In the latter case, the order just happened to be regarding a scientific theory. To put it slightly differently, in 1616, the underlying issue was the interpretation of texts; in 1633, it was a matter of obedience.

To us, the Inquisition's treatment of Galileo was unduly harsh. And no doubt it was. But compared to standard legal practice of the times, the Church proceeded "in a sufficiently objective manner with altogether exceptional consideration paid to Galileo."[30] Galileo scholar Annibale Fantoli warns us to

> avoid projecting without qualification our modern ideal of freedom of thought back to an age of increasing "absolutism," as was Galileo's time where the principle of authority (both in civil and ecclesiastical affairs and no less in the Protestant than in the Catholic camps) was considered superior to the principle of individual intellectual freedom.[31]

Just as it was possible to obtain "good" medical care in the Renaissance, a person could be treated "well" by the courts. When considering either case today, we are moved to thanksgiving.

26

THE TROJAN HORSE

Galileo left Rome on July 6, 1633, arriving in Siena three days later. For Maria Celeste, this was still too far away; she needed to look after him. In one of her letters, she wrote:

> There are two pigeons in the dovecote waiting for you to come and eat them; there are beans in the garden waiting for you to pick them. Your tower laments your long absence. When you were in Rome, I said to myself: "If he were only at Siena!" Now that you are at Siena I say: "If only he were at Arcetri!" But God's will be done.[1]

God apparently wanted Galileo in Arcetri. In December the grand duke interceded on Galileo's behalf, obtaining permission for Galileo to return to his villa in Arcetri. However, Galileo would have to "live there in solitude, without summoning anyone, or without receiving for a conversation those who might come."[2] But he was allowed to take walks in his gardens and travel to the nearby convent of Saint Matthews to visit his daughters. In fact, the Inquisition's observers apparently grew fond of Galileo and only kept track of people entering and leaving the house. In many respects, security was pleasantly lax. Nevertheless, Galileo was still a prisoner.

At Arcetri that winter, Galileo suffered a serious hernia. When he petitioned to visit doctors in Florence, the Inquisition refused, adding that if Galileo didn't stop making such requests, he would find himself in a Roman prison.[3] The grand duke could do nothing about this except provide a comforting visit in March 1634.[4]

Other than the hernia, Galileo's health was better than it had been in years. Furthermore, he was at home, close to all three of his children. But Maria Celeste had grown chronically weak during their separation. A friend of Galileo's from Pisa wrote to him:

> Most of all I am distressed by the news of Suor [i.e., Sister] Maria Celeste. I know the fatherly and daughterly affection which exists between you; I know the lofty intellect, and the wisdom, prudence, and goodness with which your daughter is endowed, and I know of no one who in the same way as she remained your unique and gentle comforter in your tribulations.[5]

When Maria Celeste became seriously ill, Galileo walked to the convent every day, "trying to hold on to her with love and prayer."[6] But on the night of April 2, Galileo received the worst news he would ever hear: Maria Celeste had died. She was only thirty-three. Galileo fell into a deep depression that nearly killed him.

Eventually he wrote to a friend:

> I held off writing you about the state of my health, which is indeed sad. The hernia has returned larger than before; my heartbeat is cut into with palpitations; immense sorrow and melancholy [accompany] loss of appetite; hateful to myself I continually hear calls from my beloved daughter . . . in addition to which I am not a little frightened by constant wakefulness.[7]

His friend, the archbishop of Siena, wrote: "I have known for a long time that she was the greatest good Your Lordship had in this world and of such towering personal importance as to merit more than paternal love."[8] That summer, Galileo relayed to a friend in Paris the events surrounding Maria Celeste's death:

> Here I lived on very quietly, frequently paying visits to the neighboring convent, where I had two daughters who were nuns and whom I loved dearly, but the eldest in particular, who was a woman of exquisite mind, singular goodness, and most tenderly attached to me.[9]

The previous year at Siena, Archbishop Piccolomini had encouraged Galileo to resume his work on motion in order to get Galileo's mind off his troubles. Galileo now turned to the same remedy in the wake of Maria Celeste's death. Eventually, Galileo was able to preoccupy himself with his work. It was finally time to write his work on terrestrial physics. And, for all he knew, he had little time left. So, despite failing health and advanced age, Galileo got to work.

While Galileo worked on motion, some of his other works were being translated or published outside of Italy. In 1634, the philosopher, theologian, and mathematician Friar Marin Mersenne (a friend of René Descartes) translated Galileo's early work *Mechanics* into French. In December 1635, the English philosopher Thomas Hobbes visited Galileo after reading an English translation of the *Dialogue*. Hobbes was one of England's most zealous proponents of an atomistic and mechanical worldview. The following year, Galileo's *Letter to the Grand Duchess* was published in Latin, giving it a widespread, albeit mainly academic, audience. Since the time of his telescopic discoveries, Galileo had been famous throughout Europe; he was now becoming legendary.

~

In February 1637, Galileo finally finished his life's work on motion—*Discourses and Mathematical Demonstrations Concerning Two New Sciences*. And none too soon. In July he lost the sight in his right eye. Within months he was completely blind. He would never actually see the published version of *Two New Sciences*; he would merely hold it in his weathered hands.[10]

Blindness is a heavy burden for anyone to bear, but perhaps more so for Galileo, whose work had been built upon observation. Dictating a letter to a friend in Paris, he lamented:

> Alas, your friend and servant Galileo has for the last month
> been irremediably blind, so that this heaven, this earth, this
> universe which I, by my remarkable discoveries and clear
> demonstrations had enlarged a hundred times beyond what
> has been believed by wise men of past ages, for me is from
> this time forth shrunk into so small a space as to be filled by
> my own sensations.[11]

Although his research had finally come to an end, his musings
had not. Even on his deathbed he would begin to dictate a third
dialogue.

Galileo's body was quickly deteriorating, and in February
1638, he again petitioned the Inquisition for permission to travel
to Florence for medical care. After all, he had nothing to lose.
This time he received permission, but only after a local Inquisitor
paid a surprise visit to make sure Galileo was truly sick. Once the
Inquisitor—and the doctor with him—saw Galileo, it was clear
he wasn't pretending.[12] He traveled to Florence, where he stayed
with his son, Vincenzio. But while there, he still needed permission to attend Mass during Holy Week, and only on the condition
that he speak with no one.

In the spring of 1638, *Two New Sciences* was published in
Leiden, Holland. This was something of a surprise, because the
Inquisition had prohibited Galileo from publishing anything ever
again. In the dedication of *Two New Sciences*, Galileo explained
how he had sent a copy of the manuscript to his dear friend and
former pupil François de Noailles, in order to preserve the work.
To his surprise, Galileo heard that Louis Elzevir in Holland had

published it. Although this had not been Galileo's intention, he was flattered and took this as a sign of Noailles's admiration.[13]

Very few scholars think that this is how it happened, the real story being much more complicated. But even so, it appears that Galileo wasn't entirely aware of how his friends were handling his manuscript.[14] Whatever the case, we can be sure he was pleased with the outcome. But we have to relegate to legend the exciting tale of Galileo smuggling his manuscript under the watchful eyes of the Inquisition's observers.

The ever-faithful Castelli reported to Galileo that *Two New Sciences* had arrived in Rome and that—surprise of surprises— Church officials permitted it to be sold.[15] This was probably because *Two New Sciences* didn't mention Copernicanism. Even Cardinal Barberini, the pope's nephew, asked for a copy.

~

For the last quarter century (since 1609), Galileo had concentrated on the heavens—on the cosmology of Copernicanism. His work on terrestrial physics had been interrupted by his astounding telescopic discoveries. But the two subjects—cosmology and physics—needed merging; the new cosmology required a new physics. If the earth was in motion, the old Aristotelian physics simply collapsed. Without a new theory of how physical objects behave on a tilt-a-whirl planet, the Copernican theory could never be reasonably accepted.

So, by making Copernicanism more plausible, *Two New Sciences* was Galileo's Trojan horse. Perhaps this was not intentional. In any event, only together would the *Dialogue* and *Two*

New Sciences work. Like soul mates, only then would they be complete.

Using the same format as the condemned *Dialogue*, Galileo wrote *Two New Sciences* as a dialogue, dividing the book into four days, and reuniting the same three men: Salviati (as Galileo's main spokesman), Simplicio (as the paradigmatic Aristotelian), and Sagredo (the intelligent, interested, but uncommitted layman).

During the first two days, the men discuss Galileo's first new science, the *science of matter*. By Galileo's time, engineers had amassed practical information on the behavior of different materials, but there was no real theory to explain this information. Galileo's science provided a possible foundation. Although Galileo emphasizes the strength of materials, he is ultimately concerned with presenting a mathematical theory of atomism. Atomism, recall, is the view that all material objects are composed of tiny, perhaps indivisible, particles. The discussion touches on such topics as the divisibility of matter, whether objects are made of an infinite number of particles, the concept of a vacuum (the space in between the atoms), and the nature of infinity.

The topic of days three and four is the *science of motion*. Whereas the first science was new because it had never been a genuine science in any sense, Galileo's science of motion was new in a different way. Galileo acknowledges that there has been no shortage of books written on motion. Furthermore, these works approached motion in a scientific or "axiomatic" sense: they laid out foundational principles and then deduced further results from these basic laws. Galileo's science of motion is new partly because of its *methods*—mathematics and experiments.

But during the discussion, Simplicio the Aristotelian struggles with the mathematics. And though in between "days," he returns home to study some Euclid, he is never up to speed mathematically and so remains mostly quiet throughout the discussion.[16] Galileo is making an obvious point: to understand the new science, you must understand mathematics. This reiterates Galileo's point from *The Assayer*: anyone who doesn't understand mathematics is incapable of evaluating many of Galileo's scientific views. This includes both philosophers and theologians.

In addition to new methods, Galileo's science of motion has a new *goal*. Unlike Aristotelian science, Galileo's doesn't search for fundamental causes. For example, it would refrain from seeking the underlying cause of an object's fall—whether this cause be an object's nature or a mysterious force that acts without contact (i.e., gravity). Salviati says:

> The present does not seem to be the proper time to investigate the cause of the acceleration of natural motion concerning which various opinions have been expressed by various philosophers . . . Now, all these fantasies, and others too, ought to be examined; but it is not really worthwhile.[17]

Better to keep it simple for now, remaining content with mathematically describing falling objects. Newton would follow this advice. And so will we.

Ironically, despite the newness of his sciences, Galileo considered himself an Aristotelian.

To be truly Peripatetic—that is, an Aristotelian philosopher—consists principally in philosophizing in conformity
with Aristotelian teachings . . . among which one is the avoidance of fallacies of reasoning . . . As to that one, I believe I
have learned sureness of demonstration from the innumerable advances made by pure mathematicians, never fallacious.
Thus far, then, I am Peripatetic.[18]

This is a backhanded compliment. Aristotelians cannot avoid fallacies by remaining fully Aristotelian. They must, says Galileo,
move from *verbal* logic to *mathematical* logic. This is the best way
to reason in natural philosophy. This is one of the main tenets of
the new sciences. It is, in effect, a new scientific method.

27

DEATH AND REHABILITATION

The young English poet John Milton visited Galileo at Arcetri in the fall of 1638. We do not know why. But a few years later, when England mandated that all publications obtain state permission, Milton wrote a tract in favor of free speech.[1] And although Milton would describe the cosmos in his epic poem *Paradise Lost*, he would be rather coy about whether it is a Copernican or Aristotelian universe.

A year later, in October 1639, probably at the grand duke's suggestion, Galileo had a young mathematics student, Vincenzio Viviani, come to live with him as an amanuensis. Viviani would later become the grand duke's mathematician, and in 1666 he would be one of the eight founding members of the Academy of Sciences in Paris.

In October 1641, Evangelista Torricelli also moved in with Galileo. Torricelli was a brilliant student of Castelli's, and Galileo was delighted to have someone with whom to talk shop. Torricelli had come to Galileo's attention earlier that year during Castelli's long-awaited visit. Castelli brought with him Torricelli's book, pointing out to Galileo what his discoveries had made possible.[2] Torricelli would be Galileo's immediate successor as the grand duke's mathematician.

And good old Castelli. Throughout the years, he had been Galileo's faithful supporter. He had spent months petitioning the Inquisition for permission to visit Galileo.[3] The Inquisition was reluctant to let him, though a now respected Benedictine abbot, see his old friend; Protestants like Hobbes and Milton, on the other hand, seem to have been let through with little difficulty.[4] In any case, Galileo touchingly wrote to Castelli:

> Bereft of my powers by my great age and even more by my unfortunate blindness and the failure of my memory and other senses, I spend my fruitless days which are so long because of my continuous inactivity and yet so brief compared with all the months and years which have passed; and I am left with no other comfort than the memory of the sweetness of former friendships, of which so few are left, although one more undeserved than all the others remains: that of corresponding in love with you.[5]

When Torricelli moved in, Galileo—blind and decrepit—was still ready to get down to work. Although he could no longer make observations or perform experiments, he could still use his mind (although even that, he complained, was failing him). Despite his extremely poor health, Galileo began dictating a new dialogue from his bed.

In November, only a month after Torricelli had arrived, Galileo came down with a fever and severe kidney pains. What bothered him most about this, he said, was that he was no longer allowed to drink wine, what he had always called "light held together by moisture."[6]

He continued dictating his dialogue nonetheless. The topic was mathematics; in particular, his reflections on two definitions from Euclid's *Elements*: the definition of *same ratio* in Book 5, and that of *compound ratio* in Book 6. These two concepts had made possible Galileo's use of mathematics to describe the physical world. On his deathbed, therefore, Galileo had returned to his roots. His work had come full circle.

Galileo never completed his dialogue on proportions. On January 8, 1642—the year Newton was born—his body finally succumbed to a lifetime of illness and gradual decay. Viviani and Torricelli were by his side; so was his son, Vincenzio. Vincenzio later wrote of his father, with the appropriate and understandable admiration of a loyal son:

Galileo was of jovial aspect, in particular in old age, of proper and square stature, of robust and strong complexion, and such that is necessary to support the really Atlantic efforts he endured in the endless celestial observations. His eloquence and expressiveness were admirable; talking seriously he was extremely rich of sentences and deep concepts; in the pleasing discourses he did not lack wit and jokes. He was easily angered but more easily calmed. He had an extraordinary memory, so that, in addition to the many things connected to his studies, he had in mind a great quantity of poetry and in particular the better parts of *Orlando Furioso* . . . His most detested vice was the lie, maybe because with the help of the mathematical science he knew the beauty of the Truth too well.[7]

Just as Galileo and his father, Vincenzio, had grown close during the latter's twilight years, so, too, did Galileo and his father's namesake. Galileo's life had come full circle.

~

Despite Galileo's immense popularity in Italy and the rest of Europe, his death and burial were largely ignored.[8] Only a few relatives, friends, and followers attended his funeral, fearing that Church officials would object to a conspicuous funeral.[9] Galileo had wished to be buried next to his father in the Basilica of Santa Croce in Florence. Instead, his body was placed in a small chamber under the church's bell tower.[10] When the grand duke planned a mausoleum for Galileo, the pope warned that although Galileo died a "good Catholic," it would be improper to honor a man who had been "vehemently suspected of heresy."[11]

But in 1983, Pope John Paul II told a group of scientists that the 350 years since Galileo's trial had allowed the Church to see the limits of its authority, and

thus is it understood more clearly that divine Revelation, of which the Church is guarantor and witness, does not involve as such any scientific theory of the universe and the assistance of the Holy Spirit does not in any way come to guarantee explanations which we might wish to maintain on the physical constitution of reality.[12]

This is close to Galileo's position on the interpretation of the two texts; namely, that the subject of Scripture and that of the Book of Nature are distinct and therefore cannot conflict. The Roman Catholic position had drastically changed. What had caused it?

Simply put, the balance of evidence for Copernicanism had shifted. The evidence for the earth's motion around the sun eventually outweighed the evidence for the geocentric interpretation of Scripture. The man primarily responsible for this was born on a small manor farm in England the same year Galileo died. Isaac Newton, combining experiment with mathematics, brought to fruition the scientific revolution Copernicus had begun. In 1687, Newton published his masterpiece, *The Principia*, and in it his "system of the world," a system of natural philosophy whose degree of coherence and accuracy had never been seen. Newton's universal laws—especially the law of gravity—applied to the heavens *and* the earth, thereby finally uniting the cosmos into a single realm, a universe. As fame of Newton's system spread, so did belief in Copernicanism (though not nearly as fast as one might think—Copernicanism didn't trickle down to common opinion until near the end of the eighteenth century).

In 1737, ten years after Newton's death, Galileo's tomb was finally built, near Michelangelo's and Machiavelli's tombs in Saint Croce's basilica.[13] (As Galileo's body was moved from the little room under the bell tower to the new mausoleum, one of his vertebrae, a tooth, and three of his fingers were taken as souvenirs.[14] One of the fingers was soon recovered; it is on display at the *Museo di Storia del Scienza* in Florence. The tooth and other two fingers were finally showcased in 2009.[15])

But the Catholic Church still officially disapproved of Copernicanism and felt a growing pressure to change its mind. In 1741, under the influence of Pope Benedict XIV, the Church finally granted Galileo's *Dialogue* an *Imprimatur*. The book, however, was given a preface indicating that Copernicanism may only be used as a mathematical tool and was not to be considered as genuinely true.[16]

With this step in the right direction, Benedict urged the Church to do more. The Holy Office relented—to some extent—and had heliocentric works from the *Index* removed in 1758; all of them except the works of Galileo and Copernicus. The Inquisition was not yet ready to admit that it had made a mistake.[17] Now, however, Catholics could wholeheartedly accept Newtonianism.[18] Finally, in 1822, Pope Pius VII intervened, and the Holy Office quietly had *De Revolutionibus* and the *Dialogue* removed from the next edition of the *Index*, published in 1835 (the *Index* itself was finally abolished in 1966).[19] The Catholic Church had finally—and fully—accepted Copernicanism.

≈

But through the years, the perceived relationship between science and religion had become strained, to put it mildly. The Enlightenment of the eighteenth century had put a premium on science while simultaneously rejecting ecclesiastical authority.[20]

Galileo's trial was a perfect example, many Enlightenment think-
ers said, of the obscurantism and heavy-handed authoritarianism
of the Church. During the Enlightenment, Galileo had come
to be seen as a secular "freethinker" (a common euphemism for
"unbeliever") and "martyr of science."[21] This myth spread like a
weed, only harder to kill.

Although the Second Vatican Council in the 1960s mentioned the Galileo affair, it was only in passing while discussing
the Catholic Church's place in contemporary culture. The
Church still made no official pronouncements on the affair. But
it was apparent that some closure was needed.

In 1979—in celebration of the centenary of Einstein's
birth—Pope John Paul II gave a speech to representatives of
both sides of the science/religion issue. On the one hand, there
was the Pontifical Academy of Sciences, an institution that saw
itself as the descendent of the Lyncean Academy. On the other
was the College of Cardinals. The pope admitted that Galileo
"had suffered much from ecclesiastical men and institutions."[22]
Two years later, in 1981, the pope formed an interdisciplinary
commission to investigate the Galileo affair in order to "remove
from many minds the blockage which that affair still puts in the
way of a fruitful concord between science and faith, Church and
world."[23] Eleven years later, in 1992, the Commission reported to
the pope, in summary:

> It is in that historical and cultural framework, far removed
> from our own times, that Galileo's judges, incapable of dis-
> sociating faith from an age-old cosmology, believed, quite

wrongly, that the adoption of the Copernican revolution, in fact not yet definitely proven, was such as to undermine Catholic tradition and that it was their duty to forbid its being taught. This subjective error of judgment, so clear to us today, led them to a disciplinary measure from which Galileo "had much to suffer." These mistakes must be frankly recognized, as you, Holy Father, have requested.[24]

Although the Commission's report fell short of many people's expectations,[25] the Catholic Church clearly accepted a certain amount of responsibility for Galileo's misfortunes. Around the world, newspapers and news stations reported that, after three- and a half centuries, the Catholic Church had finally rehabilitated Galileo.

The pope, in response to the Commission's report, spoke to both scientists and theologians, warning that there was always the possibility of a new Copernican case and that, in such a case, both sides need "to have an informed awareness of the field and limits of their own competencies."[26] But, the pope went on to say:

It is a duty for theologians to keep themselves regularly informed of scientific advances in order to examine, if such be necessary, whether or not there are reasons for taking them into account in their reflection or for introducing changes in their teaching.[27]

"Paradoxically," said the pope, "Galileo, a sincere believer, was more perceptive in this regard than the theologians who opposed him."[28] In fact, the Roman Catholic Church has acknowledged that Galileo was correct regarding many of the exegetical principles found in his *Letter to the Grand Duchess*. It should come as no great surprise that the Catholic Church eventually judged Galileo to be correct on these matters. Galileo was, for the most part, repeating what St. Augustine had written centuries earlier.

It is primarily the duty of Catholic scientists, said the pope, to competently judge when a scientific claim should be accepted. To the Pontifical Academy he said:

> And the purpose of your Academy is precisely to discern and to make known, in the present state of science and within its proper limits, what can be regarded as an acquired truth or at least as enjoying such a degree of probability that it would be imprudent and unreasonable to reject it. In this way unnecessary conflicts can be avoided.[29]

This is, perhaps, a plea for scientists to be careful about the standards that a scientific claim must meet. This was one of the mistakes that Galileo had made: he lost sight of the fact that Copernicanism didn't meet his own standards of science.

The main issue, therefore, is a matter of carefully weighing the evidence—the evidence for a scientific theory and the evidence for the meaning of a biblical passage. In this sense, scientific theories and biblical interpretations will always hang in the balance. And the balance is a lever, a simple machine. Like Archimedes, Galileo would no doubt approve of the metaphor. And we have come full circle.

NOTES

PREFACE
1. James Reston Jr., *Galileo: A Life* (Washington, D.C.: Beard Books, 2000), 9.
2. See for example, Stillman Drake, *Galileo: A Very Short Introduction* (Oxford: Oxford University Press, 2001), 9–10; and Dava Sobel, *Galileo's Daughter: A Historical Memoir of Science, Faith, and Love* (New York: Walker & Company, 1999), 17.
3. Reston, *Galileo: A Life*, 8–9.
4. Vincenzo Galilei, *Dialogue on Ancient and Modern Music*, trans. Claude V. Palisca (New Haven: Yale University, 2003), 12.
5. Ibid., xxvii.
6. Specifically, Book VIII of his *Physics* (Ibid., 12). Vincenzio was probably referring to 8.3 (254a). Galilei, *Dialogue on Ancient and Modern Music*, 12, fn. 16.
7. Galilei, *Dialogue on Ancient and Modern Music*, xxviii.
8. Ibid., xxviii.
9. Drake, *Galileo: A Very Short Introduction*, 116.
10. Ibid., 117.
11. Ibid., 115.

CHAPTER 1: FROM MONKS TO MEDICINE
1. Michael Sharratt, *Galileo: Decisive Innovator* (Cambridge: Cambridge University Press, 1994), 22–23.
2. Stillman Drake, *Galileo at Work: His Scientific Biography* (New York: Dover Publications, Inc., 1978), 448.
3. Ibid., 1.
4. Sobel, *Galileo's Daughter*, 17.
5. Annibale Fantoli, *Galileo: For Copernicanism and for the Church*, trans. George V. Coyne, 3rd ed., vol. 6, Studi Galileiani (Vatican City: Vatican Observatory Publications, 2003), 38.
6. Stillman Drake, "Vincenzio Galilei," in *Dictionary of Scientific Biography*, ed. Charles Coulston Gillispie (New York: Charles Scribner's Sons, 1972), 249.

7. Fantoli, *Galileo*, 38; Drake, *Galileo at Work*, 1.
8. Reston, *Galileo: A Life*, 6.
9. J. J. Fahie, *Galileo: His Life and Work* (London: John Murray, 1903), 7.
10. Allan-Olney, *The Private Life of Galileo: Compiled Principally from His Correspondence and That of His Eldest Daughter*, 15.
11. Leonardo Olschki, "Galileo's Literary Formation," in *Galileo: Man of Science*, ed. Ernan McMullin (New York: Basic Books, 1967), 140.
12. Sobel, *Galileo's Daughter*, 17.
13. Drake, *Galileo at Work*, 2.

CHAPTER 2: AN ADVANCED CIVILIZATION
1. Paul F. Grendler, *The Universities of the Italian Renaissance* (Baltimore: The Johns Hopkins University Press, 2002), 179.
2. Sara Bonechi, *How They Make Me Suffer . . . A Short Biography of Galileo Galilei*, trans. Anna Teicher (Florence: Institute and Museum of the History of Science, 2008), 13.
3. Sharratt, *Galileo: Decisive Innovator*, 26.
4. Ibid., 34.
5. Thomas S. Kuhn, *The Copernican Revolution: Planetary Astronomy in the Development of Western Thought* (Cambridge: Harvard University Press, 1957), 101.
6. Drake, *Galileo: A Very Short Introduction*, 1.

CHAPTER 3: EVERYTHING IN ITS RIGHT PLACE
1. David C. Lindberg, *The Beginnings of Western Science: The European Scientific Tradition in Philosophical, Religious, and Institutional Context, Prehistory to A.D. 1450*, 2nd ed. (Chicago: University of Chicago Press, 2007), 39–40.
2. Kuhn, *The Copernican Revolution*, 87.
3. Herbert Butterfield, *The Origins of Modern Science: 1300-1800* (New York: Free Press, 1957), 15.

CHAPTER 4: THE SEDUCTION
1. Drake, *Galileo at Work: His Scientific Biography*, 2–3.
2. Reston, *Galileo: A Life*, 14.

CHAPTER 5: "IGNORANCE OF MOTION IS IGNORANCE OF NATURE"
1. Drake, *Galileo at Work*, 3.
2. Bonechi, *How They Make Me Suffer*, 17.

3. Drake, *Galileo at Work*, 21.
4. 200b14–15.
5. 200b12.

CHAPTER 6: A WORLD OF MACHINES

1. Drake, *Galileo at Work*, 4–5.
2. Ibid., 5.
3. Ibid.
4. Bonechi, *How They Make Me Suffer*, 17.
5. Pietro Redondi, "From Galileo to Augustine," in *The Cambridge Companion to Galileo*, ed. Peter Machamer (Cambridge: Cambridge University Press, 1998), 187.
6. From *La Balancetta*, quoted in Laura Fermi and Gilberto Bernardini, *Galileo and the Scientific Revolution* (Mineola: Dover Publications, 2003), 114.
7. Heath, vol. 2, 18.
8. See Peter Machamer, "Galileo's Machines, His Mathematics, and His Experiments" in *The Cambridge Companion to Galileo*, ed. Peter Machamer (Cambridge: Cambridge University Press, 1998).
9. Machamer, "Galileo's Machines, His Mathematics, and His Experiments," 64.
10. Ibid., 57.
11. Peter Machamer, ed. *The Cambridge Companion to Galileo*, 16.

CHAPTER 7: THE GEOMETRY OF HELL

1. Fantoli, *Galileo: For Copernicanism and for the Church*, 43.
2. Reston, *Galileo: A Life*, 19.
3. William R. Shea and Mariano Artigas, *Galileo in Rome: The Rise and Fall of a Troublesome Genius* (Oxford: Oxford University Press, 2003), 15.
4. Richard G. Olson, *Science & Religion, 1450–1900: From Copernicus to Darwin* (Baltimore: Johns Hopkins University Press, 2004), 58.
5. Robert S. Westman, "The Copernicans and the Churches," in *God & Nature: Historical Essays on the Encounter Between Christianity and Science* (Berkeley: University of California Press, 1986), 93.
6. Olson, *Science & Religion*, 58.
7. Shea and Artigas, *Galileo in Rome*, 5.
8. Westman, "The Copernicans and the Churches," 93.
9. Ibid.
10. Shea and Artigas, *Galileo in Rome*, 5.

11. Reston, *Galileo: A Life*, 19.
12. Shea and Artigas, *Galileo in Rome*, 15.
13. Drake, *Galileo at Work* 14.
14. Shea and Artigas, *Galileo in Rome*, 13.
15. Ibid., 14.
16. Ibid., 15.
17. Ibid.
18. Kuhn, *The Copernican Revolution*, 111.
19. Drake, *Galileo: A Very Short Introduction*, 1.
20. Kuhn, *The Copernican Revolution*, 112.
21. Ibid., 112.
22. Ibid., 2.
23. Reston, *Galileo: A Life*, 26.
24. Drake, *Galileo at Work*, 14. The leading Catholic theologian, Robert Bellarmine, says, "There is no doubt that it is indeed reasonable that the place of devils and wicked damned men should be as far as possible from the place where the angels and blessed men will be forever." William R. Shea, "Galileo and the Church," in *God & Nature*, 125.
25 Drake, *Galileo at Work*, 14.
26. Ibid., 14.
27. Reston, *Galileo: A Life*, 23.
28. Sharratt, *Galileo: Decisive Innovator*, 43–4.
29. Reston, *Galileo: A Life*, 23.
30. Stillman Drake, "Galileo's Pre-Paduan Writings: Years, Sources, Motivations," in *Essays on Galileo and the History and Philosophy of Science* (1999), 221.
31. Ibid., 221.

CHAPTER 8: TORTURING NATURE

1. Drake, *Galileo at Work*, 17.
2. Ibid., 16.

CHAPTER 9: IN THE SHADOW OF THE LEANING TOWER

1. Sharratt, *Galileo: Decisive Innovator*, 45.
2. Sobel, *Galileo's Daughter*, 19.
3. Sharratt, *Galileo: Decisive Innovator*, 61.
4. Reston, *Galileo: A Life*, 29.
5. Drake, *Galileo: A Very Short Introduction*, 21.

6. Reston, *Galileo: A Life*, 33.

7. Sharratt, *Galileo: Decisive Innovator*, 52.

8. Drake, *Galileo at Work*, 20.

9. Drake, *Galileo: A Very Short Introduction*, 22.

10. John Losee, *A Historical Introduction to the Philosophy of Science*, 4th ed. (Oxford: Oxford, 2001), 23.

11. Ernan McMullin, *Galileo: Man of Science* (New York: Basic Books, 1967), 18.

12. Sharratt, *Galileo: Decisive Innovator*, 60.

13. Sobel, *Galileo's Daughter*, 21.

14. Reston, *Galileo: A Life*, 45.

15. Ibid., 45.

CHAPTER 10: PADUAN PLEASANTNESS

1. Grendler, *The Universities of the Italian Renaissance*, 40.

2. Fantoli, *Galileo: For Copernicanism and for the Church*, 55.

3. Drake, *Galileo: A Very Short Introduction*, 25.

4. Sharratt, *Galileo: Decisive Innovator*, 63.

5. Stillman Drake, "Galileo Galilei," in *Dictionary of Scientific Biography*, ed. Charles Coulston Gillispie (New York: Charles Scribner's Sons, 1972), 247.

6. Ibid., 247–48.

7. McMullin, *Galileo: Man of Science*, 4.

8. Sharratt, *Galileo: Decisive Innovator*, 71.

9. Fantoli, *Galileo: For Copernicanism and for the Church*, 56–57.

CHAPTER 11: EARTH DISPLACED

1. Westman, "The Copernicans and the Churches," 85.

2. Fantoli, *Galileo: For Copernicanism and for the Church*, 59.

3. Sharratt, *Galileo: Decisive Innovator*, 69.

4. Fantoli, *Galileo: For Copernicanism and for the Church*, 58.

5. Stillman Drake, *Discoveries and Opinions of Galileo* (New York: Anchor Books, 1957), 241.

6. Fantoli, *Galileo: For Copernicanism and for the Church*, 61.

CHAPTER 12: AN ILL WIND

1. Sharratt, *Galileo: Decisive Innovator*, 66.

2. Drake, *Galileo: A Very Short Introduction*, 30.

3. Drake, *Galileo at Work*, 45.

4. Sharratt, *Galileo: Decisive Innovator*, 73.

5. Drake, *Galileo at Work*, 47.

6. Sharratt, *Galileo: Decisive Innovator*, 73.

7. Fantoli, *Galileo: For Copernicanism and for the Church*, 55.

8. Ibid., 55–6.

9. Kuhn, *The Copernican Revolution*, 199.

10. J. Blötzer (1910), "Inquisition," in *The Catholic Encyclopedia* (New York: Robert Appleton Company) http://www.newadvent.org/cathen/08026a.htm.

11. Ibid.

12. Westman, "The Copernicans and the Churches," 86.

13. Ibid., 86.

14. Shea and Artigas, *Galileo in Rome*, 118.

15. Sobel, *Galileo's Daughter*, 23.

16. Ibid., 25.

17. Drake, *Galileo at Work*, 51.

18. Sobel, *Galileo's Daughter*, 26.

19. Drake, *Galileo at Work*, 51.

20. Ibid., 74–75.

21. Ibid., 74.

22. Ibid., 75.

23. Sobel, *Galileo's Daughter*, 22.

24. Drake, *Galileo at Work*, 76.

25. Barry Gower, *Scientific Method: An Historical and Philosophical Introduction* (New York: Routledge, 1997).

CHAPTER 13: A STAR IS BORN

1. Drake, *Galileo at Work*, 104; Fantoli, *Galileo: For Copernicanism and for the Church*, 65.

2. Drake, *Galileo at Work*, 104.

3. Ibid., 105.

4. Ibid., 106.

5. Ibid., 118.

6. Ibid.

7. Sharratt, *Galileo: Decisive Innovator*, 83.

8. Drake, *Galileo: A Very Short Introduction*, 44.

9. Ibid.

10. Sobel, *Galileo's Daughter*, 30.

11. Drake, *Galileo: A Very Short Introduction*, 46.

CHAPTER 14: DESEGREGATION

1. Drake, *Galileo at Work*, 190.
2. Ibid., 138.
3. Ibid., 139.
4. Ibid., 141.
5. Ibid.
6. Drake, *Galileo: A Very Short Introduction*, 43.
7. Drake, *Galileo at Work*, 142
8. Sharratt, *Galileo: Decisive Innovator*, 17.
9. Drake, *Discoveries and Opinions of Galileo*, 23.
10. Shea and Artigas, *Galileo in Rome*, 44.
11. Drake, *Discoveries and Opinions of Galileo*, 36.
12. Ibid., 36, fn. 9.
13. Steven Shapin, *The Scientific Revolution* (Chicago: University of Chicago Press, 1996), 19.
14. Fantoli, *Galileo: For Copernicanism and for the Church*, 85.
15. Reston, *Galileo: A Life*, 100.
16. Ibid., 100.
17. Fantoli, *Galileo: For Copernicanism and for the Church*, 86.
18. Ibid., 88.
19. Drake, *Galileo at Work*, 158.
20. Ibid., 165.
21. Fantoli, *Galileo: For Copernicanism and for the Church*, 97.
22. Drake, *Galileo at Work*, 164–5.
23. Ibid., 168–69.
24. Sharratt, *Galileo: Decisive Innovator*, 18.
25. Drake, *Galileo at Work*, 158–9.
26. Reston, *Galileo: A Life*, 103.
27. Drake, *Galileo at Work*, 160–1.
28. Sobel, *Galileo's Daughter*, 36.

CHAPTER 15: THE PAX ROMANA

1. Sobel, *Galileo's Daughter*, 38.
2. Ibid., 37.
3. Ibid., 38.
4. Ibid., 38–9.
5. Fantoli, *Galileo: For Copernicanism and for the Church*, 97.
6. Allan-Olney, *The Private Life of Galileo*, 55.
7. Fantoli, *Galileo: For Copernicanism and for the Church*, 95.

8. Ibid., 96–97.
9. Noel M. Swerdlow, "Galileo's Discoveries with the Telescope and Their Evidence for the Copernican Theory," in *The Cambridge Companion to Galileo*, ed. Peter Machamer (Cambridge: Cambridge University Press, 1998), 261.
10. Drake, *Galileo at Work*, 163–64.
11. Richard S. Westfall, *Essays on the Trial of Galileo*, vol. 5, Studi Galileiani (Vatican City State: Vatican Observatory Publications, 1989), 11.
12. Drake, *Galileo at Work*, 164.
13. Kuhn, *The Copernican Revolution*, 202.
14. Drake, *Galileo: A Very Short Introduction*, 56.
15. Shea and Artigas, *Galileo in Rome*, 29.
16. Ibid., 31.
17. Fantoli, *Galileo: For Copernicanism and for the Church*, 102.
18. This is, in fact, Drake's main thesis in his book, *Galileo: A Very Short Introduction*.
19. Fantoli, *Galileo: For Copernicanism and for the Church*, 104.
20. Shea and Artigas, *Galileo in Rome*, 35.
21. Fantoli, *Galileo: For Copernicanism and for the Church*, 103.
22. Sharratt, *Galileo: Decisive Innovator*, 92.
23. Giorgio de Santillana, *The Crime of Galileo* (Chicago: University of Chicago Press, 1955), 75.
24. Ibid.
25. Ibid., 74.
26. Westfall, *Essays on the Trial of Galileo*, 6.
27. Sharratt, *Galileo: Decisive Innovator*, 91.
28. Ibid., 92.
29. Shea and Artigas, *Galileo in Rome*, 39.
30. Ibid., 39.
31. Ibid., 45.

CHAPTER 16: A NEW FRIEND

1. Sobel, *Galileo's Daughter*, 44.
2. Olson, *Science & Religion*, 18.
3. Reston, *Galileo: A Life*, 125.
4. Shea and Artigas, *Galileo in Rome*, 46.
5. Sobel, *Galileo's Daughter*, 44–45.
6. Ibid., 44.

7. Sharratt, *Galileo: Decisive Innovator*, 95.
8. Sobel, *Galileo's Daughter*, 86.
9. Sharratt, *Galileo: Decisive Innovator*, 98.
10. Drake, *Galileo at Work: His Scientific Biography*, 209.
11. Ibid., 213.

CHAPTER 17: THE THEOLOGICAL TURN

1. Shea and Artigas, *Galileo in Rome*, 48.
2. Fantoli, *Galileo: For Copernicanism and for the Church*, 126.
3. Drake, *Galileo at Work*, 197.
4. Fantoli, *Galileo: For Copernicanism and for the Church*, 128.
5. Westman, "The Copernicans and the Churches," 80.
6. Kuhn, *The Copernican Revolution*, 107.
7. Sharratt, *Galileo: Decisive Innovator*, 73.
8. Drake, *Galileo: A Very Short Introduction*, 68.
9. Fantoli, *Galileo: For Copernicanism and for the Church*, 128.
10. Ibid.
11. Ibid.
12. Verses 12–13, The New American Standard Bible, 1995 Update (La Habra, California: The Lockman Foundation), 1996 (emphasis added).
13. Drake, *Galileo: A Very Short Introduction*, 69.
14. Maurice A. Finocchiaro, *The Essential Galileo* (Indianapolis: Hackett Publishing Company, 1989), 104.
15. Ibid.
16. Ibid.
17. John 3:12, NASB.
18. Finocchiaro, *The Essential Galileo*, 106.
19. Ibid., 104.
20. Ibid., 105.

CHAPTER 18: WARNING SIGNS

1. Fantoli, *Galileo: For Copernicanism and for the Church*, 125.
2. Sobel, *Galileo's Daughter*, 66.
3. Fantoli, *Galileo: For Copernicanism and for the Church*, 135.
4. Ibid., 426, fn. 8.
5. Ibid., 131.
6. Sharratt, *Galileo: Decisive Innovator*, 110.
7. Ibid.
8. Ernan McMullin, "Galileo on Science and Scripture," in *The Cambridge*

Companion to Galileo, ed. Peter Machamer (Cambridge: Cambridge University Press, 1998), 281.

9. Maurice A. Finocchiaro, *The Galileo Affair: A Documentary History* (Berkeley: University of California Press, 1989), 134.

10. Ibid., 135.

11. Ibid.

12. Sharratt, *Galileo: Decisive Innovator*, 111.

13. Fantoli, *Galileo: For Copernicanism and for the Church*, 134.

14. Finocchiaro, *The Galileo Affair*, 58.

15. Fantoli, *Galileo: For Copernicanism and for the Church*, 169.

16. Ibid.

17. Ibid., 170.

18. Finocchiaro, *The Essential Galileo*, 146.

19. Verses 4–6, NASB.

20. Finocchiaro, *The Essential Galileo*, 147.

21. McMullin, "Galileo on Science and Scripture," 273.

22. Finocchiaro, *The Essential Galileo*, 147.

23. Ibid.

24. Ibid.

CHAPTER 19: THE CRUX

1. Giorgio Spini, "The Rationale of Galileo's Religiousness," in *Galileo Reappraised*, ed. Carlo L. Golino (Berkeley: University of California Press, 1966), 66.

2. Finocchiaro, *The Essential Galileo*, 147.

3. Ibid., 119.

4. McMullin, "Galileo on Science and Scripture," 296.

5. Thomas Dixon, *Science and Religion: A Very Short Introduction* (Oxford: Oxford University Press, 2008), 18.

6. Finocchiaro, *The Essential Galileo*, 126.

7. Ibid.

8. Fantoli, 2003 #51, 368.

9. Finocchiaro, *The Essential Galileo*, 137–38.

10. Ibid., 114.

11. Fantoli, *Galileo: For Copernicanism and for the Church*, 194.

12. Finocchiaro, The Essential Galileo, 140.

CHAPTER 20: COPERNICUS MAKES THE LIST

1. Shea and Artigas, *Galileo in Rome*, 74.

2. Ibid., 76.

3. Spini, "The Rationale of Galileo's Religiousness," 58.

4. Shea and Artigas, *Galileo in Rome*, 79.

5. Ibid., 75.

6. Ibid.

7. Fantoli, *Galileo: For Copernicanism and for the Church*, 174.

8. Ibid., 176–77.

9. Shea and Artigas, *Galileo in Rome*, 81.

10. Fantoli, *Galileo: For Copernicanism and for the Church*, 175.

11. Ibid., 175.

12. Shea and Artigas, *Galileo in Rome*, 81.

13. Ibid., 81–82.

14. Sharratt, *Galileo: Decisive Innovator*, 129.

15. Ibid., 130.

16. Shea and Artigas, *Galileo in Rome*, 91.

17. Drake, *Galileo: A Very Short Introduction*, 82.

18. Shea and Artigas, *Galileo in Rome*, 85.

19. Ibid., 85–86.

20. Ibid., 87.

21. Fantoli, *Galileo: For Copernicanism and for the Church*, 186.

22. Shea and Artigas, *Galileo in Rome*, 89–90.

23. Ibid., 90.

CHAPTER 21: ESCAPING THE LABYRINTH

1. Fantoli, *Galileo: For Copernicanism and for the Church*, 200.

2. Peter Machamer, "Galileo Galilei," in *The Stanford Encyclopedia of Philosophy*, ed. Edward N. Zalta (Stanford: Center for the Study of Language and Information, 2009).

3. Sobel, *Galileo's Daughter*, 93.

4. Drake, *Discoveries and Opinions of Galileo*, 227.

5. Ibid., 227.

6. Sharratt, *Galileo: Decisive Innovator*, 137.

7. Finocchiaro, *The Essential Galileo*, 183.

8. Ibid., 188.

9. Shea and Artigas, *Galileo in Rome*, 119.

10. Robert E. Butts, "Galileo," in *A Companion to the Philosophy of Science*, ed. W. H. Newton-Smith, Blackwell Companions to Philosophy (Oxford: Blackwell, 2001), 151–52.

11. Drake, *Galileo at Work*, 284.

12. Shea and Artigas, *Galileo in Rome*, 108.
13. Ibid., 128.
14. Sobel, *Galileo's Daughter*, 4.
15. Sharratt, *Galileo: Decisive Innovator*, 151.

CHAPTER 22: NEW HOPE
1. Reston, *Galileo: A Life*, 189–90.
2. Fantoli, *Galileo: For Copernicanism and for the Church*, 214.
3. Ibid., 215.
4. Sobel, *Galileo's Daughter*, 99.
5. Ibid., 107.
6. Ibid.
7. Sharratt, *Galileo: Decisive Innovator*, 144.
8. Stillman Drake, "Galileo and the Church," in *Essays on Galileo and the History and Philosophy of Science* (1999), 162.
9. Ibid.
10. Ibid.
11. Ibid.
12. Shea, "Galileo and the Church," 128.
13. Shea and Artigas, *Galileo in Rome*, 131.
14. Spini, "The Rationale of Galileo's Religiousness," 47.
15. Shea and Artigas, *Galileo in Rome*, 131.
16. Ibid., 131–32.

CHAPTER 23: THE DIALOGUE
1. Drake, "Galileo and the Church," 163.
2. Drake, *Galileo: A Very Short Introduction*, 88.
3. Fantoli, *Galileo: For Copernicanism and for the Church*, 243.
4. Ibid., 244.
5. Ibid.
6. Ibid., 245.
7. Ibid.
8. Ibid., 244.
9. Ibid., 246.
10. Ibid.
11. Drake, "Galileo and the Church," 163.
12. Ibid., 164.
13. McMullin, *Galileo: Man of Science*, 35.
14. Fantoli, *Galileo: For Copernicanism and for the Church*, 247.

15. Shea and Artigas, *Galileo in Rome*, 146.
16. Drake, "Galileo and the Church," 163.
17. Drake, *Galileo at Work*, 314.
18. Ibid., 336.
19. Shea and Artigas, *Galileo in Rome*, 157.
20. Fantoli, *Galileo: For Copernicanism and for the Church*, 252.
21. Drake, *Galileo at Work*, 336.
22. Shea and Artigas, *Galileo in Rome*, 127.
23. Galileo Galilei, *Dialogue Concerning the Two Chief World Systems: Ptolemaic and Copernican*, ed. Stephen Jay Gould, trans. Stillman Drake, The Modern Library Science Series (New York: The Modern Library, 2008), 6.
24. Ibid., 257.
25. Ibid., 57.
26. Ibid., 295.
27. Ibid., 381.
28. Shea and Artigas, *Galileo in Rome*, 125.
29. Galilei, *Dialogue Concerning the Two Chief World Systems: Ptolemaic and Copernican*, 225.
30. Ibid., 272.
31. Shea and Artigas, *Galileo in Rome*, 121.
32. McMullin, *Galileo: Man of Science*, 41.
33. Ibid., 34.
34. Sharratt, *Galileo: Decisive Innovator*, 169.
35. Galilei, *Dialogue Concerning the Two Chief World Systems: Ptolemaic and Copernican*, 538.
36. Ibid., 538.

CHAPTER 24: "AN OUTBURST OF RAGE"

1. Drake, *Galileo at Work*, 337.
2. Ibid., 337.
3. Ibid., 343.
4. Fantoli, *Galileo: For Copernicanism and for the Church*, 341.
5. Drake, *Galileo at Work*, 338.
6. Shea and Artigas, *Galileo in Rome*, 164.
7. Drake, *Galileo at Work*, 338.
8. Galileo Galilei and Maurice A. Finocchiaro, *Galileo on the World Systems: A New Abridged Translation and Guide* (Berkeley: University of California Press, 1997), 82.
9. Shea and Artigas, *Galileo in Rome*, 173.

10. Drake, *Galileo at Work*, 339.

11. Shea and Artigas, *Galileo in Rome*, 174.

12. Reston, *Galileo: A Life*, 237.

13. Drake, *Galileo at Work*, 340.

14. de Santillana, *The Crime of Galileo*, 198.

15. Fantoli, *Galileo: For Copernicanism and for the Church*, 499, fn. 44.

16. Drake, *Galileo at Work*, 339–40.

17. Ibid., 348.

18. Fantoli, *Galileo: For Copernicanism and for the Church*, 343.

19. Drake, "Galileo and the Church," 164.

20. Drake, *Galileo at Work*, 342.

21. Ibid., 342.

22. Shea, "Galileo and the Church," 132.

23. Drake, *Galileo at Work*, 343.

Chapter 25: Vehement Suspicion of Heresy

1. Shea and Artigas, *Galileo in Rome*, 183.

2. Drake, *Galileo at Work*, 346. See also Finocchiaro, *The Galileo Affair*, 259.

3. Drake, *Galileo at Work*, 347. See also Finocchiaro, *The Galileo Affair*, 259.

4. Drake, *Galileo at Work*, 340–41.

5. Shea and Artigas, *Galileo in Rome*, 188.

6. Finocchiaro, *The Galileo Affair*, 278.

7. Maurice A. Finocchiaro, "That Galileo Was Imprisoned and Tortured for Advocating Copernicanism," in *Galileo Goes to Jail: And Other Myths About Science and Religion*, ed. Ronald L. Numbers (Cambridge: Harvard University Press, 2009), 77.

8. Ibid., 71–72.

9. Drake, *Galileo at Work*, 351.

10. Ibid., 351.

11. Finocchiaro, "That Galileo Was Imprisoned and Tortured for Advocating Copernicanism," 73.

12. Fantoli, *Galileo: For Copernicanism and for the Church*, 332.

13. Ibid., 332–33.

14. Drake, *Galileo at Work*, 288.

15. Ernan McMullin, ed., *The Church and Galileo* (Notre Dame: University of Notre Dame Press, 2005), 5.

16. Shea and Artigas, *Galileo in Rome*, 196.
17. Ibid., 197.
18. Drake, *Galileo: A Very Short Introduction*, 114.
19. Drake, *Galileo at Work*, 417.
20. Ibid., 417.
21. Ibid.
22. Ibid., 418–19.
23. Drake, *Galileo: A Very Short Introduction*, 115.
24. Shea and Artigas, *Galileo in Rome*, 194.
25. Fantoli, *Galileo: For Copernicanism and for the Church*, 337.
26. Shea and Artigas, *Galileo in Rome*, 195.
27. Finocchiaro, "That Galileo Was Imprisoned and Tortured for Advocating Copernicanism," 68.
28. Shea and Artigas, *Galileo in Rome*, 195.
29. Drake, *Galileo at Work*, 351–52.
30. Fantoli, *Galileo: For Copernicanism and for the Church*, 334.
31. Ibid., 335.

CHAPTER 26: THE TROJAN HORSE

1. Allan-Olney, *The Private Life of Galileo*, 262.
2. Ibid., 345.
3. Sharratt, *Galileo: Decisive Innovator*, 181.
4. Ibid., 181.
5. Sobel, *Galileo's Daughter*, 344.
6. Ibid., 345.
7. Drake, *Galileo: A Very Short Introduction*, 99–100.
8. Sobel, *Galileo's Daughter*, 345.
9. Ibid., 347.
10. Fantoli, *Galileo: For Copernicanism and for the Church*, 347.
11. Drake, *Galileo: A Very Short Introduction*, 107.
12. Sharratt, *Galileo: Decisive Innovator*, 186.
13. Ibid., 184.
14. Drake, *Galileo: A Very Short Introduction*, 103.
15. Fantoli, *Galileo: For Copernicanism and for the Church*, 347.
16. Sharratt, *Galileo: Decisive Innovator*, 202.
17. Galileo Galilei, *Dialogues Concerning the Two New Sciences*, ed. Robert Maynard Hutchins, *Great Books of the Western World* (Chicago: William Benton, 1952), 202.
18. Drake, *Galileo: A Very Short Introduction*, 109.

CHAPTER 27: DEATH AND REHABILITATION

1. Sobel, *Galileo's Daughter*, 350–51; and Michael Segre, "The Never-Ending Galileo Story," in *The Cambridge Companion to Galileo*, ed. Peter Machamer (Cambridge: Cambridge University Press, 1998), 393.

2. Sharratt, *Galileo: Decisive Innovator*, 207.

3. Drake, *Galileo at Work*, 416.

4. Ibid., 416.

5. Sobel, *Galileo's Daughter*, 361.

6. Drake, *Galileo at Work*, 421.

7. Sobel, *Galileo's Daughter*, 359.

8. Segre, "The Never-Ending Galileo Story," 389.

9. Ibid., 409, fn. 11.

10. Paolo Galluzzi, "The Sepulchers of Galileo: The 'Living' Remains of a Hero of Science," in *The Cambridge Companion to Galileo*, ed. Peter Machamer (Cambridge: Cambridge University Press, 1998), 418.

11. Drake, *Galileo at Work*, 436.

12. Fantoli, *Galileo: For Copernicanism and for the Church*, 368.

13. Ibid., 351.

14. Sobel, *Galileo's Daughter*, 366.

15. http://www.huffingtonpost.com/2009/11/20/giovanni-targioni-tozzett_n_365455.html.

16. McMullin, ed., *The Church and Galileo*, 6.

17. Ibid.

18. Sharratt, *Galileo: Decisive Innovator*, 209.

19. McMullin, ed., *The Church and Galileo*, 6.

20. Segre, "The Never-Ending Galileo Story," 396.

21. Ibid., 398.

22. Sharratt, *Galileo: Decisive Innovator*, 212.

23. Ibid.

24. Ibid., 218.

25. McMullin, ed., *The Church and Galileo*, 2.

26. Sharratt, *Galileo: Decisive Innovator*, 218–19.

27. Ibid., 220.

28. Ibid., 219.

29. Ibid., 222.

ACKNOWLEDGMENTS

Thomas Nelson has continued its excellent track record of giving me helpful and cheerful guidance. I'm particularly grateful for my editor, Kristen Parrish. And special thanks to my wife, Christine, the second person to read the entire book (I'm pretty sure I was the first). Christine helpfully pointed out where it seemed as if she was the first to read it.

ABOUT THE AUTHOR

Mitch Stokes is a Fellow of Philosophy at New St. Andrews College, where he teaches philosophy, logic, mathematics, and science, reuniting them into a single discipline. He received his PhD in philosophy from Notre Dame and an MA in religion from Yale. He also holds an MS in mechanical engineering and, prior to his philosophy career, worked for an international engineering firm where he earned five patents in aeroderivative gas turbine technology. He and his wife, Christine, have four children.

Close Encounters of the Christian Kind

— Available Now —

JANE AUSTEN
9781595553027

**ANNE
BRADSTREET**
9781595551092

**WILLIAM F.
BUCKLEY**
9781595550651

JOHN BUNYAN
9781595553041

**WINSTON
CHURCHILL**
9781595553065

ISAAC NEWTON
9781595553034

**SAINT
FRANCIS**
9781595551078

SAINT PATRICK
9781595553038

D. L. MOODY
9781595550477

SAINT NICHOLAS
9781595551153

SERGEANT YORK
9781595550255

JOHANN SEBASTIAN BACH
9781595551085

Available August 2011

GEORGE WASHINGTON CARVER
9781595553034

J. R. R. TOLKIEN
9781595551078